CONVERSATIONS

— WITH —

Uncle Joe

HONEST DISCUSSIONS OF LIFE'S ISSUES

JOSEPH PEEK

Print ISBN: 978-1-09838-344-2

eBook ISBN: 978-1-09838-345-9

DEDICATION

This book is dedicated to every young person who is without an older adult to confide in, trust, and share their concerns about life's issues without feeling as though they're being judged. My prayer is that this book helps them find their way, so that they can do the same for someone else.

TABLE OF CONTENTS

INTRODUCTION

I discovered the power of conversation in my early teenage years. I had had a terrible argument with my mother about nothing of great consequence, but because I was going through the turbulent times of adolescence, I said some things out of the overflow of my emotions that troubled her. My words were something to the effect that it didn't matter if I was dead, no one would care. Whatever I said, it was disturbing to my mother. Later that week when my father returned from out of state, he sat me down and talked to me about my behavior and what I had said. In order to best understand the full impact of this conversation you must be introduced to my father. My dad was the pastor of one of the Baptist Churches in our small community where we lived and another church in a smaller town about an hour's drive away. He was also an English teacher at a high school in Kingstree, South Carolina. My dad was a very busy man who was well known and respected in the communities he served. It was very rare for me to be his only congregant. This had to be a big deal. He explained how much my mom loved me and the sacrifices she made daily, just for me. Like most selfish, self-centered youngsters I had no idea. I love my mother and depended on her for stability, consistency, care, everything. Deep down I was aware of my mother's love, but my father's words penetrated my heart. I cried like a baby; slobbering, nose running and I felt ashamed. This was a pivotal moment in my life regarding my relationship with my mother. From that day on, until her passing years later, I didn't argue with her or purposely cause her any concern. I decided to be better and do better, because my mom deserved better. I was by no means perfect, but I made a conscious decision to minimize emotional and mental harm to my mother. This was my first lesson of the power of conversation.

During my work career as a military recruiter and an educator I worked with hundreds, if not thousands of young people who lacked good counsel regarding some of the most basic issues in life. I once jokingly said I would record myself and play the recording for the next student I talked to who had that specific issue. This book is not a fix to the complexities of people's lives, but it is meant to be a help to the reader.

RELATIONSHIPS

Relationships are the very foundation of the human race. In the bible God said, it wasn't good for man to be alone, so He made a woman, He called Eve. He then told them, Adam and Eve, to be fruitful and multiply. There are very few people who can spend all of their time alone. Those who do, oftentimes, need therapy to regain a sense of reality and even sanity. We have various relationships with co-workers, acquaintances, girlfriends, buddies, best friends, spouses, brothers, sisters, nieces, nephews, sons, daughters, mothers, fathers, grandparents, aunts, and even uncles. Sometimes the people we love most are the hardest to get along with. I don't profess to know much, but I know my life is better, because of the various relationships I have had and have today. Every portion of this book is about relationships and how to best navigate the complexities and conflicts that are sure to arise. My hope is that each reader finds an adequate solution to at least one problem or issue that they are sure to face during this journey called life.

LOVE

Nephew (Todd): Uncle Joe, I think I'm in love with Kim, but I'm not sure.

Uncle Joe: What makes you think you're in love with her?

Todd: I can't get her out of my head. I'm always thinking about her. I love being around her.

Uncle Joe: I remember having those feelings about your Aunt Ann. Love is one of those words that people define in many different ways. It is a powerful word that can cause people to do things they wouldn't ordinarily do. I recall my mother talking to my sisters about boys and or men and how they might use the word love to convince them to have sex with them. I believe my mom was speaking to me at the same time, telling me indirectly not to use the word love to get into some girls' panties. I heard her loud and clear. In the few relationships I had, I don't remember ever telling anyone that I loved them: The only exception was the young lady who would later become my wife. I had to learn what love is. The bible says, God is love. I agree with that. Love is not an emotion. It is greater than that, it's spiritual. When I met your Aunt Ann, I didn't have a clue about love. I believe love is reflected in what I am willing to do for the person or people I say I love. Before we got married we were living thousands of miles apart. We were both in the Air Force and met while we were stationed in England. I had received orders and had been stationed in Louisiana for about six months. This was long before email, cell phones, and FaceTime, so we communicated via the postal service and by phone, which was somewhat expensive and terribly inconvenient. I felt as though she was falling in love with me, which was not a bad thing, but I wasn't sure about my feelings for her. I didn't want her to invest all her time and affection on me and end up getting hurt, so I wrote and mailed her a letter. She called it a "Dear Jane" letter. I let her know I was unsure if my feelings for her were enough to make a commitment to her. I wasn't confident that I loved her because I didn't understand what love is, but I knew I didn't want to hurt her. I learned that love is a willingness to lose a relationship with a wonderful person to prevent them from being hurt.

Yes, putting someone else before self. Love is not taking. Love is giving. If you are willing to wait until marriage to have sex or make love with her, per her request, you might be in love. If you are willing to be a better person and do your best because you know she deserves your best, you might be in love. If you are willing to give her up, for her happiness, you might be in love with her. Only you can answer those questions.

MARRIAGE

Todd: What's up Uncle Joe?

Uncle Joe: Not much. What's up with you?

Todd: Quite a bit.

Uncle Joe: How's it going with you and Kim?

Todd: I'm thinking about asking her to marry me, but I want to be sure.

Uncle Joe: I know what you mean. Before I met your Aunt Ann I asked your granddad how he knew your grandmother was "the one." At the time I was probably twenty-one years old or so. I wasn't in a serious relationship, but felt ready to settle down. All I needed to do was meet "the one." I knew your granddad, being a Baptist pastor who spoke so eloquently to the congregation with great wisdom and knowledge, was going to drop some serious knowledge on me. As I prepared to take mental notes, he opened his mouth and said, "I just knew." What? I was very disappointed with his response, because it didn't answer my question. I knew enough not to ask the next logical question, what do you mean you just knew? which is just a rephrasing of the first one. I left his presence as bewildered as before I opened my mouth.

Todd: I'm surprised. I thought granddad was a great orator. So, what did you do?

Uncle Joe: I prayed and asked God and I still almost messed things up.

Todd: How's that?

Uncle Joe: Let me start from the beginning. Shortly after that conversation God led me to the book of Genesis in the bible and said, "What was Adam doing when I saw he needed a wife or help meet?"

Todd: You heard God's voice out loud, like Moses and Abraham?

Uncle Joe: No, it was like when you have an idea or thought that comes from within. We'll talk more about that at a later time. Just trust that I knew it was God speaking to me.

Todd: Okay. I'm sorry…

Uncle Joe: No problem, but like I was saying…the answer to what Adam was doing was what God had told him to do. The part that really stood out about the question to me was, having a wife wasn't Adams idea. It was God's. The point being God knows exactly what we need. He is the one who brings your spouse to you. Somewhere in the course of time He makes sure your paths cross. Have I ever told you how I met your Aunt Ann?

Todd: No, I don't think so.

Uncle Joe: I was stationed in England. I had been there for almost two years. During this time, our unit had responsibility to rotate troops in and out of Germany on two to three-week schedules. I had just returned from one of those rotations. I attended church that Sunday, as was my practice, and I noticed a couple of young ladies had joined our congregation and choir. Your Aunt Ann was one of them. While hanging up our robes, I introduced myself to her. She said hello and told me her name, but didn't seem interested in carrying on a conversation.

Todd: Oh, so she was playing hard-to-get or giving you the cold shoulder.

Uncle Joe: No, she told me later that the chow hall was about to close and she didn't want to miss that meal. She was a little thing back then. She couldn't afford to miss a meal.

Todd: So, what happened next.

Uncle Joe: Our church group participated in church services in different parts of England. The church leaders would lease nice buses with the big windows to transport those who wanted to go. On this particular occasion they rented two buses. On the way to the event your Aunt Ann and her friends were on the other bus. Once we got to Fairford, that was the name of the town or air base, we began to mingle a bit. When it was time to leave, one of her friends came on the bus where I was and asked me if I wanted to ride with them, on their bus. I knew what they were up to so I said yes. The seat reserved for me just happened to be beside your Aunt Ann. I sat down and we began to talk. I was twenty-three years old and thought your Aunt Ann was about my age. As we began to talk she mentioned something about just graduating from high school months earlier, so I asked her how old she was. She said she was eighteen years old. Jokingly, I stood up and said I can't talk to you, you're too young. What she said next made me more interested in getting to know her.

Todd: Okay…what did she say.

Uncle Joe: She said, "Well go on then – bye," or something like that. I was impressed by her response. She wasn't some airhead, but had a sense of who she was, at the age of 18, soon to be 19. She wasn't a silly little girl, but a young lady. I sat back down and our conversation continued. All the way back we talked and laughed. We laughed so hard we cried. I had never had so much fun talking to anyone before, especially not a young lady.

Todd: Wow.

Uncle Joe: After that we became very close. She was the first young lady who I could really talk to. She listened to me and her responses were filled with wisdom and knowledge beyond her years. I had a couple of months or so left in England before I had to report to my next duty station in Louisiana. We were together "all the time," per her friends. I loved being around her. When I was with her I hated to leave and when I wasn't with her, I look forward to our next meeting.

Todd: That sounds like me with Kim.

Uncle Joe: That's a good sign. The time for me to leave came and she was the last person I saw before my departure. She hugged and held me tight, while crying with her head resting on my shoulder. She apologized for slobbering on my nice sweater. She and I were both surprised by her overflow of emotions. I didn't know how much she cared for me, nor did I realize I was in love with her until weeks later, as I imagined her sitting beside me as I drove to various locations. A little over a year after I left England she came to Louisiana where we would get married, but being a typical man, I had cold feet. I just didn't want to make a mistake and mess up her life or mine.

Todd: Of course, you worked things out, but what was the problem?

Uncle Joe: I was scared. Marriage is a big commitment. Fortunately, I had a talk with the mutual friend Ann was staying with in Louisiana during her visit and God used that young lady to get me over my fear(s). During our conversation she said a lot, but what spoke to me was the answer to the question, "Can you live with her (Ann)?" I know it sounds so simple, but for me that was the question that I had to answer, and the answer was yes! She was already my confidant and best friend. I'll add this at no additional charge.

Todd: What's that?

Uncle Joe: My love for Ann had little to do with her physical beauty.

Todd: A friend of mine married this beautiful, fine, gorgeous girl he met in grad school, but he says he is just now seeing her beauty. I thought bro are you blind? It sounds like what you are saying, cause Aunt Ann is still an attractive woman. I bet she was fine back in the day.

Uncle Joe: Yeah, I look at old pictures and can appreciate the beauty she was and still is. There's nothing wrong with noticing a young lady's beauty first. That was the norm for me back then, but with Ann I fell in love with who she really is before acknowledging her looks. So back to your question of being sure about asking Kim to marry you. Can you live with her?

Todd: Yes, Sir! I see some similarities in your relationship with Aunt Ann and ours. I really can't see a future without her. She makes me want to be a better man. She encourages me and never puts me down.

Uncle Joe: That's important.

Todd: She, like Aunt Ann, is very capable, intelligent, focused, kind, caring, loving, compassionate...I could go on and on.

Uncle Joe: Sounds like she's a keeper. Are you able to take care of her financially?

Todd: Yes Sir, I'm doing well on the job and have started my own business on the side that is very promising.

Uncle Joe: Excellent! I'm one of those guys who loves being married. Hopefully you'll be a member of this club. As long as you both are willing to work at it, because it does take work, you'll be just fine. Make sure you send an invitation to your Aunt Ann. She likes weddings. You can put my name on it too. I might come along with her.

Todd: Alright Uncle Joe, I'll let you know.

THE WEDDING

Uncle Joe: One more thing.

Todd: What's that?

Uncle Joe: Make sure you two don't get caught up in the wedding. Sometimes people, especially young ladies, get caught up in the idea of the wedding and spend too much money, get all stressed out and all of that and can't enjoy the process. I hope I don't sound sexist, but that's been my observation. The wedding is the event or ceremony that initiates the marriage officially. You have the wedding so you can be married.

Todd: Doesn't everybody know that?

Uncle Joe: Well, based on some of what I have seen, no. Too many couples focus on the wedding to put on a big show. In my opinion, that's not what it's supposed to be about. If you want it to be extravagant and you can afford it there's nothing wrong with that. The emphasis, again, should be on the marriage after the wedding and honeymoon, if you take a honeymoon immediately after. It's like so much emphasis is put on the wedding that they forget about the marriage and all of what is involved in it. Where are you going to live? Do you have furniture, dishes, appliances? How are we going to handle our money?

Todd: That's a lot to consider.

Uncle Joe: It is...and I'm not saying you have to have all of this spelled out completely, but the wedding is what you have to do to be married and being married is the primary thing.

Todd: Okay, I see what you're saying. So how did you and Aunt Ann get married?

Uncle Joe: We got married at the courthouse in Alexandria, Louisiana.

Todd: Why? We don't have any family down there, do we?

Uncle Joe: No. No family was in attendance. We had three ladies who worked at the courthouse volunteer to be witnesses. You know how some women love that romantic stuff.

Todd: Why Louisiana?

Uncle Joe: Because of our circumstance of being stationed thousands of miles apart and needing to use the system to help us get stationed together once Ann's time was up in England. We thought it best to get married. Our emphasis was on getting married. Your Aunt Ann has always wanted to have a wedding and we may one day, but our marriage of more than 30 years has been a wonderful experience for both of us and that's most important.

Todd: Got it. Kim and I have talked more about our possible life together more than the wedding. We are thinking of having a small, intimate event with family and close friends. This guy at work got married last year and he was complaining about the cost of the wedding, the rings, and honeymoon. I don't think they're doing well financially at least partially because of that debt.

Uncle Joe: That's what I mean. You don't want to be in that type of situation. The first years of marriage can be difficult enough without having financial problems. Which brings me to another important thing to consider: How you're going to handle your money. You don't have to figure all this out now, but during your engagement period this should be discussed as well.

Todd: How do you and Aunt Ann handle your finances?

Uncle Joe: Every couple has to decide what works best for them. I handle paying the bills. I actually use a spreadsheet, so I can see where our money is going and to make sure I don't forget to pay anything. We have a bank account where our paychecks are deposited and is considered our primary bank account. I have another account that I have had since before I met Ann. She has access to that account as well. The money that we make is our money. It all goes into those two pots. That works for us. We have some good friends where the wife handles their finances. Again, it's all about what works best for the two of you.

Todd: Man...that's a lot of information.

Uncle Joe: I know, but sometimes I like to discuss things when they come to mind. As long as I'm around feel free to ask me anything you have a concern about. I know your mom and dad provide you with good counsel too.

Todd: Yes, they do, but there are some things I'd rather not discuss with them for various reasons or just want to get another perspective or confirmation of my thinking. You don't mind me using you, do you?

Uncle Joe: No, not at all.

(TWO YEARS LATER)

Todd: Hey, Uncle Joe.

Uncle Joe: What's up nephew? How's the wife doing?

Todd: She's good.

Uncle Joe: How are you enjoying being married.

Todd: It's great! I love it. Kim has started talking about wanting a baby.

Uncle Joe: How long have you been married now?

Todd: About two years.

Uncle Joe: Yeah, that sounds familiar. Your Aunt Ann and I were married about two years before she started talking about having a baby. I was thinking we'd wait about five years into the marriage before having a kid. I knew it would completely change our lives, for the rest of our lives and thought we should enjoy it just being the two of us for a little while longer.

Todd: I was thinking of waiting another year or two. So, how long were you guys married before you had Nicole?

Uncle Joe: Just over three years.

Todd: I want to have kids, but I don't know if I'm ready for that responsibility.

Uncle Joe: I know what you mean. I felt the same way, but came to understand that you are never really ready for some things, you just have to jump in and swim.

Todd: How did you deal with Aunt Ann's morning sickness.

Uncle Joe: She didn't have any of those issues. She read the scripture in the bible that says something about women being saved from the ills of child bearing and she claimed that she was included in that promise.

Todd: Maybe Aunt Ann can share that scripture with Kim.

Uncle Joe: I'm sure she will. I remember bringing Nicole home from the hospital. It was such a weird reality. We left the house and it was just the two of us. We came back home with another human being, for whom we held full responsibility for her well-being. Nicole would cry, like babies do, and we didn't know what was wrong with "it," as I recall saying at least once. I know that sounds cold, but it's the truth. We had to get used to our new world. I wouldn't change anything regarding having kids. It is one of the greatest gifts from God. I didn't know what unconditional love was until we had kids. There's nothing that they can do to make me stop loving them.

Todd: That's deep Uncle Joe.

Uncle Joe: It's true. There's nothing like taking a nap on the couch with your 6 to 9-month-old child resting on your chest or getting up in the early hours of the morning, preparing bottles and nursing your child. It's tiring, but worth every minute.

Todd: I'm sort of excited about the idea now.

Uncle Joe: I won't take any credit or blame no matter what you do or when you do it.

Todd: I know Uncle. You have a great day.

Uncle Joe: You too.

PRE-SCHOOL

Uncle Joe: Your Aunt Ann told me that as of a couple of days ago you became a daddy.

Todd: Yes, Sir!

Uncle Joe: Congratulations! It's time to start Preschool!

Todd: What do you mean, preschool?

Uncle Joe: I mean exactly what I said. Pre-school begins no later than at birth. Some might say before birth…reading and singing to the child while they're still in the womb. The idea of pre-school is to prepare the child for school, academically, socially, and emotionally. The child is learning whether you are teaching intentionally or not.

Todd: Well I get that.

Uncle Joe: I have heard it said that parents are their child's first teachers.

Todd: Okay, I agree with that.

Uncle Joe: I guess the question is what kind of teacher are you going to be? Too many parents judge teachers harshly while their child is in the school system, but don't take their responsibility seriously enough before their kid gets to kindergarten.

Todd: I never heard it put quite like that.

Uncle Joe: Have I ever told you about my first-grade experience?

Todd: No, but that was a long time ago. Can you remember back that far?

Uncle Joe: Yes, I can and it's relevant to our conversation. By the way, you can put a hold on the shade you are throwing my way…

Todd: Sorry, Uncle Joe. You know I can't help it. It's a part of who I am.

Uncle Joe: You might want to check yourself before you walk away from here with a black eye or a punch in your throat!

Todd: Yes, Sir. I'll do better. So, you started school in first-grade? What happened to kindergarten?

Uncle Joe: I don't know. Just before I entered first grade I went to a "head-start" program for a few weeks. That did little to prepare me for what my teacher expected from her students. I remember not being able to write my name. I think I knew the alphabets, but I had not been taught how they should be arranged to spell my name. Most of the kids in my neighborhood were in my class. My best friend's mom, who was an elementary school teacher, had taught him these basic skills.

Todd: Why didn't grandma or grandpa teacher you?

Uncle Joe: Like you said, it was a long time ago; during the Civil Rights Movement. Your grandparents were consumed with survival and keeping us safe. Dad was pastoring two churches and teaching full-time out of state. I think his involvement in the civil rights movement in the local area made it difficult for him to find a job in the county. It was just the circumstance in which I found myself. I believe, when we know better, we have a responsibility to do better. I survived my early years of public education and haven't really looked back, as far as regrets go. I had to work harder my first few years in school because I was behind, but I caught up and have done fairly well for myself, by God's grace.

Todd: You have a couple of master's degrees, right?

Uncle Joe: No, just one. I said all of that to try to emphasize the importance of pre-school. If I had been provided with what my kids, your cousins, where provided with it would have made a great difference. Of course, your Aunt Ann can take about 90% of the credit for their "pre-schooling." A child's self-esteem can be damaged, sometimes beyond repair, when they experience academic struggles so early. If they stay behind their peers academically and rarely, if ever, experience academic success, they may stop trying. People need someone to believe in them and encourage them. When that is lacking, especially with small children, it can be difficult for them to overcome their deficiencies.

Todd: Wow, I see what you mean about the importance of pre-school and starting early. Mom and dad both taught me so much before I entered kindergarten that I was able to skip second grade. I was reading before I started kindergarten and always have a book, newspaper, or magazine near me even today, because I love to read.

Uncle Joe: Your pre-schooling is the foundation of your early academic success. Also, I know your parents were very systematic in their approach to discipline.

Todd: Yeah, man. We had a specific time to do everything. The day was regimented. At times I thought I was in boot camp. We had meal times and had to eat everything off of our plate. We had to be in the house before the streetlights came on. We had to do our homework before we could change into our play clothes and go outside to play. We had to say please, thank you, your welcome... all of that.

Uncle Joe: "All of that" is pre-schooling. I'm sure you remember kids in your classes who were running around, not listening to the teacher, and acting up.

Todd: Yeah, this kid named Billy was always in trouble. He was so bad the kids would get mad at him, because his behavior made it more difficult for the teacher to teach.

Uncle Joe: Do you know where Billy is today?

Todd: Last I heard he was in jail. I don't know if he ever graduated high school.

Uncle Joe: You might think this is extreme, but I believe the importance of a parent's pre-schooling their children can be the difference between life or death.

Todd: You're right Uncle Joe. I never really thought of it that way, but you're right.

Uncle Joe: So, teaching your kid basic academics, proper behavior, to abide by simple rules, helps shape their future. We know there aren't any guarantees in life, but what we don't want is to have any regret for not doing what we know we ought to do. By the way all of that takes additional work by the parents. Another important part of pre-schooling is spending fun time with your kids. You need to talk to them, play with them, and take them on field trips, to include vacations. Your cousins, Dias and Nicole, can tell you how important that was for them during their pre-school years and throughout their childhood. Your Aunt Ann was taking those kids all over the Hampton Roads area when we lived there.

Todd: I'm going to call mom and dad and thank them for all they've done for me, especially my "pre-schooling."

Uncle Joe: That sounds like a great idea. Don't give my brother too much credit though. Your mom, like your Aunt Ann, did most of the work.

Todd: I'll let him know you said that.

Uncle Joe: It's the truth!

INFIDELITY

Todd: Uncle Joe, do you have a few minutes to talk.

Uncle Joe: Well, I guess I can set aside some time for my favorite nephew. What's up?

Todd: I have a new co-worker on the job and I am seriously attracted to her. She looks like a runway model and is very intelligent. We have to work together on various projects and the more I learn about her the more I'm attracted to her.

Uncle Joe: Has Kim met her?

Todd: No. Why do you ask?

Uncle Joe: Because women have this sixth sense, where they can detect emotions in the air. It's like a spiritual gift or something.

Todd: This is why I'm talking to you. I never thought I'd be attracted to another woman like this after marrying Kim. I mean Kim is my soul mate. Did you ever experience anything like this?

Uncle Joe: Yes, I have. I think it is an unfortunate condition that most men have to contend with. It's not a question of whether you love your spouse, it's an innate reality of our flesh or human nature. This is why infidelity is often a problem in marriages.

Todd: What did you do?

Uncle Joe: The first thing I had to do is realize that being married to the most wonderful, beautiful, intelligent woman in the world doesn't change that thing in me, as a man, that makes my eyes wander. I believe that is just a natural phenomenon. I am attracted to women. They are one of God's most beautiful and wonderful creations. What I must learn to do is to control my response to this "phenomenon." I had to do some self-talk and be honest with myself. This lady is beautiful, true. I'm attracted to her, true. She's not mine, true. I can't afford to lose what I have with Ann, true. I don't want to lose what I have with Ann.

The ultimate question for me was, am I willing to lose all I have with Ann to have sex with another woman? Fortunately, for me, the answer was and is no.

Todd: You make it sound easy.

Uncle Joe: I don't want to give the impression that it was no problem for me and in 30 minutes time I had settled this issue, because that's not so. In every situation that may arise, I have to use this process. I have a great relationship with Ann and I don't want to hurt her. These are things you have to remind yourself of, so that you don't fall into the lust trap. Again, I'm not dead yet, so, as old as I am, I still have to contend with this issue, though it is easier to deal with now. Human beings have animal-like instincts at times, but we also have the ability to think logically and rationally in order to make good decisions. So, it's not easy. Like everything else that's worthwhile in life, it takes work. These are some practical things that you can do:

- Admit to yourself that you find this lady attractive.

- Don't allow yourself to take your thoughts beyond that.

- Imagine what life would be like if you lost Kim.

- Considered how you would feel if Kim cheated on you. How would that affect your relationship with her?

- Practice controlling your body. One good way to do this is by fasting: Abstaining from eating food or certain types of food for a short period of time.

- Don't put yourself in a position where you have an opportunity to cheat.

- Minimize time spent alone with her and in conversation.

- Don't stop dating Kim. Have a night out and take mini vacations every so often, without the kids. This may involve dressing up and looking your best. This will help keep your relationship fresh and enjoyable.

I'm going to add this thought because I think I should. What if I have an affair?

Todd: I haven't!

Uncle Joe: Good! But what if I did. Then what? I know I would have to tell Ann eventually, because that's the kind of relationship we have. I also know it would break her heart. I would have to give her time to heal and trust me again, if she chose to stay with me. I don't want to come across as having arrived in any aspect of life. I have made several mistakes. The bible says, "all have sinned and come short of the glory of God." I'm definitely included in that scripture. We have to work daily to try to be and do better. I think one of the hardest things I'd have to do is forgive myself. Let me leave you with a biblical story of a man named Joseph. He was a Jewish young man enslaved by an Egyptian officer. The officer's wife kept trying to get Joseph to have sex with her. One day she grabbed him and he ran away, leaving his robe in her hands. She lied and said Joseph tried to have sex with her. You'll need to read the whole story for yourself, but my point is his response to the opportunity of having sex with her kept him from the act. We might want to add running from the situation to the list I mentioned earlier. I have great admiration for Joseph, because I'm sure the officer's wife was very attractive, physically. Joseph's commitment to doing the right thing was such that he wasn't going to sin no matter what. That's the standard I have to keep in front of me and aspire to.

Todd: I never thought I'd ever be attracted to another woman like this. Talking to you has helped.

Uncle Joe: Anytime you need to talk to someone, as long as I'm here, you can call on me. I'll do what I can. You know this conversation has helped me too. I need to make sure I'm practicing the things I'm sharing with you.

Todd: Thanks Uncle Joe. I appreciate you man.

Uncle Joe: I appreciate you too.

PRIORITIES

Todd: Thanks for coming over and helping me with my car.

Uncle Joe: No problem. I like working on cars on occasion and spending time with one of my nephews. If Nicole and Dias lived closer I'd probably do most of their vehicle maintenance.

Todd: I really appreciate it.

Uncle Joe: So, where's Kim and the kids?

Todd: They went to the beach with one of her girlfriends and her kids.

Uncle Joe: Why didn't you go with them?

Todd: I had too much to do.

Uncle Joe: How often do you vacation as a family?

Todd: It's very rare. I can't tell you the last time we went somewhere, vacationing as a family.

Uncle Joe: How old is your baby boy?

Todd: He's four. He'll be starting kindergarten next school year.

Uncle Joe: We really didn't start vacationing regularly until the kids were about six and ten. Before that time, we just went to visit mom and dad and Ann's family. For about three years we didn't really go anywhere because Dias didn't like being in his car seat and would cry and scream...I couldn't take it. I also had a very stressful job, was going to school part-time, and heavily involved in church.

Todd: That sounds like me right now. I'm doing a lot, so it's hard for me to find time for family stuff, especially vacations.

Uncle Joe: I thought I couldn't find time for "quality family time" either, but one day, and I can't tell you why, maybe I had a "light bulb moment" or just listened to your Aunt, but I got my priorities straight. I went to the book of Genesis, like I often do, and read about the beginning of mankind.

Todd: And what did you find?

Uncle Joe: I found that my first responsibility is my relationship with God: That I'm communing with Him on a daily basis, through prayer, reading the bible, and meditation, or being in a quiet place so I can hear from Him. My second responsibility is family...spending time with Ann and the kids.

Todd: That sounds good, but how did you do it? How do you make time, where there is no time?

Uncle Joe: Some other stuff may have to go undone or have someone else do it. For example, I could have done this work on your car or you could have taken it to the shop and had it done.

Todd: I don't like taking advantage of people or paying all that money when I can do it myself.

Uncle Joe: Well, first you should know that it's impossible to take advantage of your Uncle Joe. I don't do anything unless I want to do it. We are a lot alike. I wish I had had someone like me who I could have asked for help when I was your age. We are family. There may very well come a time when I'll need to call on you for help. I'm just paying it forward. I believe you reap what you sow. Secondly, you need to find a good mechanic in town who you trust, so you have that option.

Todd: Yeah...

Uncle Joe: Before I forget, what we were talking about, my priorities are God, family, and then everything else. When I speak of God I'm talking about my relationship with Him. I'm not talking about going to church or being a good church member, although that is a small part of the equation. When I speak of family, my relationship with Ann is a higher priority than that of my kids; because after the kids are grown and gone there's still the two of us. Some couples put their kids above their relationship with each other and years later wonder what happened. With that being said, you must spend quality time with your kids. They require your attention every day. They need to know you love and care about them and the best way to do that is to spend time with them. In retrospect, I could have done better, but I'm glad I at least did what I did. "Everything else," is just that; work, church, continuing your education, all that stuff. I know you have to pay the bills, but you'll always have bills. Your kids are only with you for a short period of time and the time you have with them is precious.

Todd: So, what did you do?

Uncle Joe: Just before I retired from the military we bought a timeshare, that allowed us to have access to vacation spots in Virginia, South Carolina, Las Vegas, Florida, and other states. We planned at least a one-week long vacation every year.

Todd: I don't know if I could do a whole week.

Uncle Joe: You may not need to, but I did. It took me the first couple of days just to come down from the stress of the job. This may sound strange, but I had to learn how to relax and enjoy vacationing. Something that helped me was that one of my supervisors had a quote on his desk that read, "Don't sweat the small stuff. It's all small stuff." That simple quote changed my life, for the better. Week-long vacations got so good to me that we started taking them twice a year, spring and summer break.

Todd: I'd have to make some serious changes. How did you afford it?

Uncle Joe: We would budget for it. Actually, before I retired from the military we started taking some trips and I would just take leave. After I retired from military service we both were working as educators, so we had the time off when the kids were off for the most part. Just as Nicole was leaving the nest we started going on cruises.

Todd: Yeah, I remember you talking about cruising.

Uncle Joe: Yeah man, in my opinion, it's the best way to vacation. All thanks to your Aunt Ann.

Todd: How's that?

Uncle Joe: We had moved to another neighborhood and had neighbors who cruised all the time. Your Aunt Ann started talking to the lady about all the fun they had and the places they went, so Ann said we're going on a cruise. I thought

I knew how it would be, so I wasn't interested at first. Ann saved the money for the cruise and months later we drove down to Florida to the port and began a vacation that proved to be the best ever. I discovered that listening to Ann and going along with her desire to cruise, was one of the wisest decisions I have ever made. I absolutely love cruising. In my opinion, it's the best way to vacation.

Todd: Yeah, I can see your enthusiasm.

Uncle Joe: Yeah man, but you have to find what works for you. The main thing is spending time with your family. We would be in the car for several hours so we'd play games, like naming states or cities by the alphabet. When we'd stop for fast food I'd say the cost is $14.26 and I'm giving them a $20 bill. How much change should I get? I found out that Dias had a great vocabulary. He'd say something and Ann and I would look at each other like, how does he know that word? That's how grown, educated people speak. I baptized Dias in a pool in Las Vegas.

Todd: What?

Uncle Joe: He asked me about baptism and he wanted to be baptized. I explained that it is a symbolic act that represents a burial of the old sinful man and the resurrection of the new. The main thing, of course is that you believe that Christ Jesus paid the price for your sins and that you accept God's gift of salvation through Jesus' death, burial, and resurrection. Baptism doesn't save you, it shows that you associate yourself with Christ, the only begotten Son of God.

Todd: Wow...I would never associate Las Vegas or any vacation with a baptism.

Uncle Joe: That's the beauty of spending time with your kids in these different environments, you don't know how it will impact them or you until you go. Vacations provided opportunities for me to get to know my kids better and for them to see me in a different light. That time spent has provided me with wonderful memories. When Dias turned 18, I asked him how his life had been thus far and he said, "it's been good, very good." I then asked him what has been the best part? He said, "the trips we've taken over the years." I love his answer because I know that that was time we spent together. I didn't have that with your grandparents, for various reasons and I longed for it. Especially from your grandad, because his work, pastoring two churches and working out of state, didn't leave much time for a family of six kids. Well, we're about finished with this car and I'm sure you're tired of hearing me talk.

Todd: No, not at all. Like you said we're family and talking to you is helpful. I needed to hear what you've said. I need to make some changes, because I'd hate to miss out on any of the experiences that you talked about with my kids. They mean the word to me...Let's clean up and go get something to eat, on me.

Uncle Joe: Sounds good.

MALE EGO

Todd: How's your chicken marsala?

Uncle Joe: Excellent, as always.

Todd: Uncle Joe, how did you deal with Aunt Ann working?

Uncle Joe: What do you mean?

Todd: How did you feel about her working?

Uncle Joe: When we met we both were active duty military, so she had a job and a career. After we got married I wanted to be able to pay for everything and let her do whatever she wanted with her money. We talked about it and the reality is her income has always allowed us to live in nicer places, have nicer things, and do more of what we wanted to do. There was a short period of time when she wasn't working full-time and I loved it. We were able to sustain our lifestyle because I was making more money by then. When she decided to go back to work full-time that was good too. How do you feel about Kim working?

Todd: I would prefer she stay home with the kids. I make enough money to take care of us fairley well.

Uncle Joe: What does she want to do?

Todd: She wants to go back to work when the baby starts kindergarten.

Uncle Joe: Again, I have experienced life with Ann working and not working; there's benefits to both scenarios. The most important thing is that she feels fulfilled. Our job as a spouse is to support one another in our becoming. If I were God I would know exactly who Ann is to become. Since I'm not God I need to trust that she is following her heart as to what she should do. For example, when Ann said she wanted to become a teacher, I supported the idea. When she had a concern about how we would finance her education, I said we'll get loans. We have to be our spouse's greatest fan and supporter. The last thing you want to do is squash your spouse's dreams.

Todd: What if she makes more money than me?

Uncle Joe: Good for her and you. It's all going in the same pot, right?

Todd: Yeah, but I'm supposed to be the breadwinner.

Uncle Joe: Only in your mind. Your wife making more money than you, doesn't diminish who you are and what you bring to the relationship. I hear what you are saying but you really need to change your way of thinking. Kim's not that kind of young lady. She's never been about being in competition with you right? Your Aunt Ann currently makes a lot more money than I do, which has allowed me the option of an early retirement. Don't limit yourself, your family's prosperity, and your wife's feeling of achievement because of your ego. I know thoughts like that come to mind and I'm glad you brought it up, because the last thing a husband needs to do is put limits on their spouse and their "righteous" ambitions. Now if they're talking crazy, that's something different, but I'm sure that's not what you have with Kim.

Todd: No, you're right. Dad told me the same thing. I just wanted to get your take on it since we're here.

Uncle Joe: No problem. I'm glad you feel like you can talk to me as well as your dad, my brother. I think it's wise to take advantage of as much good counsel as you can get. It can help you avoid problems down the road. Never let your male ego or that type of mentality lead you down that road, where there's a definite dead end of regret: Which is something you want to avoid at all cost.

REGRET

Todd: Regret?

Uncle Joe: Yes! I can't imagine being my age, kids grown and gone and not having these memories. I would be miserable. Also, if I hadn't supported and encouraged Ann to go back to school and get her bachelor's degree.

Todd: Yeah, because that's allowed you to retire early, right?

Uncle Joe: Yes, but more importantly she wouldn't be the person she is today. She wouldn't have the options or opportunities that are available to her. She wouldn't be a few months away from completing her doctorate degree, nor have been in the positions of influence, over these past years, to make a difference in so many people's lives .

Todd: What regrets do you have, if any?

Uncle Joe: Fortunately, I only have a couple or at least that's all that comes to mind. The summer before I started my senior year in high school your grandparents move about 30 minutes away from where we had lived all of my life. I begged them to find a way for me to be able to finish high school with my friends. A wonderful lady named Mrs. Moore stepped up and said I could stay with her during the school year. She had also paid me $20 to cut her grass before. That was a lot of money back then. So, I'm a 17, then 18-year-old knucklehead, consumed with self and never took the opportunity to tell her how much I appreciated all she had done for me.

Todd: Why didn't you tell her?

Uncle Joe: Shortly after I graduated she passed away, but I had plenty of time to thank her. She passed before I matured enough to do better. She didn't have to open her home to me, but she did so, out of the kindness of her heart. Another regret is the last time I had the opportunity to talk to a good friend, I didn't take it and during my travels, while in the military, he passed away. By the time I was made aware of his death two years had passed. I couldn't believe it.

Todd: Why do you think you didn't say something in both situations, other than as you say you were a knucklehead?

Uncle Joe: I struggled with low self-esteem as a kid and as a young man, which is no excuse. That may have had something to do with it. Maybe I didn't think my words would matter. I have long since learned to give "flowers," as they say, to folks while they can enjoy their beauty and fragrance. As we live, hopefully we learn and can apply that knowledge to our lives. Perhaps then, seeing the positive results, we can pass that knowledge on to someone else.

Todd: Like you have done today...Well, I got my car fixed and a boat load of stuff to think about. I'm going home and calling Kim and the kids.

Uncle Joe: I'm going to go home and take a nap! I didn't like taking naps so much as a kid, but I love them as an older man.

Todd: I might do that too. Thanks Uncle Joe. Love you man.

Uncle Joe: Love you back. Tell the family I said hello.

FRIENDSHIP

Uncle Joe: Hey niece, how are you doing?

Niece (Mollie): Not so good.

Uncle Joe: Sorry to hear that. What's going on?

Mollie: You know Tonya, right?

Uncle Joe: Yes. Isn't she your best friend?

Mollie: She was.

Uncle Joe: What happened?

Mollie: It's like she dropped me for this other girl, who doesn't even like me.

Uncle Joe: How long have you and Tonya been friends?

Mollie: About ten years.

Uncle Joe: Wow…So it's obvious that this is bothering you.

Mollie: Yeah, we were very close.

Uncle Joe: Friendship is one of those things in life that can be seasonal or temporary. I have people in my life who I haven't seen or spoken to for years, who I still consider friends. My best friend (in childhood) was my neighbor who lived across the street from us. I remember as a little kid, being so happy to see another little boy, living close to us. Years later, as adults, with grown children of our own, we were having a conversation and I told him that he was my best friend when we were kids. He said he didn't have any best friends as a child.

Mollie: What?

Uncle Joe: No…He wasn't being mean or insensitive. He was being honest. I didn't take offense to his response, because I understand. He was that guy that everybody wanted to be around. He's just good people, from good people. His mom was like a second mother to me. She allowed me to escape from my four sisters on several occasions, which I greatly appreciated.

Mollie: Oh, okay.

Uncle Joe: So, one person's expectations or definition of friendship or being best friends can be totally different and it's okay. While we are on the subject of friendship(s), don't be too quick to consider a person a friend.

Mollie: Yes, I know about that. I used to think everybody was my friend, but learned that very few people are actually friends; most are acquaintances. I guess that's why this thing with Tonya is bothering me.

Uncle Joe: Do you still consider her a friend?

Mollie: Yes…I guess I can keep her in that category. Thanks Uncle Joe.

Uncle Joe: No problem.

SECRETS, LIES, TRUTHS

Uncle Joe: Abby, why are you so upset? It looked like if I hadn't rolled up when I did you and Jasmine would have been throwing hands (fighting).

Niece (Abby): I would have pulled that weave out of her head.

Uncle Joe: I thought you two were friends.

Abby: I thought we were too, but she can't seem to keep my name out of her mouth.

Uncle Joe: What do you mean?

Abby: The reason I confronted her…

Uncle Joe: Oh, so you confronted her.

Abby: Yes, because she put some stuff on social media about me.

Uncle Joe: Okay, let's go get a soda, ice cream, or something so you can calm down before we talk about this…

…You seem to be a lot calmer now.

Abby: I am. I don't like it when people do stuff like that.

Uncle Joe: You said she put some information on social media about you right?

Abby: Yeah.

Uncle Joe: Now that you are calm, I want you to listen closely to what I'm about to say.

Abby: Okay.

Uncle Joe: You can't stop people from talking about you. If I confronted everyone that said something about me that I didn't like, I wouldn't have time to do much else; and I'm not as popular as you. Whenever someone says something about you it's either the truth or a lie. Which one was it?

Abby: It was a lie! I didn't say or do what she said I did.

Uncle Joe: Have you ever known Jasmine to lie?

Abby: Yes, she told me something about Candice and Junior that I found out wasn't true. That was two separate incidents.

Uncle Joe: Liars lie. It's what they do. I can't explain it…I once worked with this guy who had stories about every topic we'd bring up in our shop. He had learned to fly a plane with the civil air patrol, been to multiple places around the world, taken martial arts and had a Black Belt. You name it he had done it. When he would tell these stories, I believed him. I had never been around anyone who lied all the time, so this was new to me. One day one of my co-workers said, "you know he's lying right? Every time we bring up a subject he has a better story than the one being told." I began to pay closer attention to what my co-worker said. This guy's lies eventually caught up with him as he couldn't keep his stories straight. Again, liars lie. It's just what they do. Now that you know Jasmine has this problem, you have to decide how you are going to handle your "friendship."

Abby: I can't be friends with someone who lies all the time. Friendship is supposed to be about trust and relying on that person to have your back, no matter what.

Uncle Joe: So, moving forward what specific actions are you going to take?

Abby: I'm not sure. I might text her and let her know we're definitely not friends and that she doesn't have to worry about me confronting her again, because I feel sorry for people who lie like that. That's sick!

Uncle Joe: That sounds like a plan. One more question, was any of what she said true?

Abby: Well, maybe a little bit. I had told her something that she knew was a secret, but she put that out there too.

Uncle Joe: How much of that had to do with why you were so upset.

Abby: Probably 90%. Friends aren't supposed to tell other friend's secrets. That's just not right.

Uncle Joe: Who do you think is most responsible for the secret getting out?

Abby: What do you mean? She is!

Uncle Joe: Don't get upset with me, but listen. If I have a secret and I tell you and you tell my brother, your dad, who is really at fault?

Abby: I am, because you told me it was a secret.

Uncle Joe: No, I am. I was the first one to break the rule or standard that I expected you to uphold. I was the first perpetrator or violator of my own rule. If I had not broken my own rule in telling you, my brother would never know and you wouldn't be involved. We have to take responsibility and own up to the fact that a secret stays a secret as long as I keep my mouth shut. I have to be honest with myself first. Don't blame someone else for something you didn't do.

Abby: When you put it like that, I guess you're right.

Uncle Joe: Now, of course, all secrets shouldn't be kept.

Abby: Like what?

Uncle Joe: If you know someone is being hurt or abused or plans on hurting or abusing someone, you can't keep that secret. You have to tell someone who can help the, would be, victim, even if your relationship with that person ends after you tell.

Abby: That's hard...

Uncle Joe: Doing the right thing isn't always easy. Sometimes it takes courage.

Abby: Yeah, because snitches get stitches.

Uncle Joe: Every person has to decide how they're going handle these types of situations for themselves, but doing the right thing helps me sleep well at night, regardless of what someone else might think or say. Let's get you home so you can start on your homework.

BULLYING

Uncle Joe: Hey, Brenda. What have you been up to?

Niece (Brenda): Not much, but if this girl keeps bullying me, I don't know...

Uncle Joe: What is she doing?

Brenda: She makes fun of my clothes, the way I look, everything.

Uncle Joe: That can be tough. I have a few minutes if you'd like to talk about it.

Brenda: Okay.

Uncle Joe: You know I have to tell you a story, right?

Brenda: I sort of like your stories.

Uncle Joe: Good! You might need to have a talk with your brother. He doesn't seem to enjoy them.

Brenda: He does. He's just trying to be "hard."

Uncle Joe: When I was a kid we didn't define bullying the way it's defined today. Bullying was physical or at least the threat of physical harm was made. Unfortunately, I had to deal with both situations. When I was in the 4th grade I recall being "bullied" by this kid, who's name I can still remember. For some unknown reason this kid kept picking on me. That's what we called it when there were just words exchanged. He just wouldn't stop pointing out any and every flaw he perceived I had. I was a skinny fellow so I guess he thought he could get away with saying anything he wanted about me, without consequence. One day, and I can't tell you how long it took me to come to this realization, I used what one might call psychology and took my power back.

Brenda: What did you do?

Uncle Joe: It was like I had a mental pause or an epiphany, questioning why I was letting this less than perfect person, point out things about me while he had imperfections too.

Brenda: I'm still stuck on the word epiphany.

Uncle Joe: That's like a light bulb moment, similar to what you see in some of the older cartoons where the character's thoughts are in a circle by their head.

Brenda: You mean like in comic books?

Uncle Joe: Yes, kind of like that.

Brenda: Okay…

Uncle Joe: So, like I was saying, the thought occurred to me, why am I allowing this person to pick out things about me that he thinks is funny? He has imperfections too. I noticed that he had big ears, so I said something like, "Well at least I don't have ears like Dumbo."

Brenda: You mean that Disney elephant that can fly?

Uncle Joe: Yeah. I noticed when I said that the tables turned. He got upset and started defending the size of his ears saying stuff like, "I don't have big ears." Amazingly, he left me alone after that. I guess you could say, I took my power back. Another time, when I was in the 9th grade, this kid who I thought was my friend decided I was going to be his victim that day. He kept hitting me and saying, "you're not going to do anything about it, you're a punk." He wouldn't stop so I told him, "hit me one more time and you'll see what happens after class." He hit me one more time. It only happened this one day, but because it involved him touching or hitting me it definitely would be defined as old school bullying.

Brenda: What did you do?

Uncle Joe: We met right outside the building after class and squared up. He pushed me and I think he thought I was going to just push him back, but I punched him in the face and kept swinging for his face. I was landing some punches, so he picked me up and held me over this railing with about a 20-foot drop. I held on to him thinking if I go down you're coming with me.

Brenda: Man, Uncle Joe, so you actually threw some hands.

Uncle Joe: Hands and I would have thrown feet too, if needed.

Brenda: You know that's hypocritical, right? You adults are always telling us not to fight.

Uncle Joe: Maybe, but sometimes a person has to physically defend him or herself. I felt like this was one of those times. The fighting I'm against is meeting someone somewhere to fight because they said something about you. That's like if I had fought the kid who was picking on me when I was in the fourth grade, it didn't justify my getting into a physical altercation. That's not a reason to fight. If I had that kind of mentality my last fight wouldn't be decades ago, but months ago, because people don't stop talking about you when they turn 21, 30, 40, or even 50 years old. You have to learn how to handle any given situation. It took a lot for me to fight this kid. He pushed me into a "corner" and I came out swinging, literally.

Brenda: So, what happened next?

Uncle Joe: A teacher broke up the fight and sent us to our next class.

Brenda: You didn't get suspended?

Uncle Joe: No.

Brenda: I bet grandma beat your behind.

Uncle Joe: No. I don't remember ever talking to her about it. I'm pretty sure she would have understood because she told me that when she was young she'd rather fight than fuss. Your grandmother was something else. The only family member that I know who knew about it was your Aunt Trish. This is long before cell phones were invented. I was surprised she was aware of the fight, because she was at the high school at the time.

Brenda: I thought you said you were in the 9th grade. Didn't you go to the same high school?

Uncle Joe: The high school was still relatively new, so it couldn't accommodate freshmen at that time. A year or two later freshmen began their high school years there.

Brenda: What happened with the other kid?

Uncle Joe: Strangely enough, we were back to how we were before the incident. I think he gained a new respect for me and learned a couple of valuable lessons.

Brenda: Like what?

Uncle Joe: Just because a person is quiet, nice, the pastor's son, about the same size as you, etc., doesn't mean he is a punk, scared, weak, frail, or lacks the ability to defend himself. You might want to leave those folks alone. I learned that I have a limit to where I will allow someone to push me and I will do what I have to in order to protect myself. Strangely, in retrospect, at no time was I upset with this kid.

Brenda: Come on Uncle Joe. There you go using those big words again. What does retrospect mean?

Uncle Joe: Looking back in reflection. That's why it's good that you talk to me. You can increase your vocabulary a little.

Brenda: I might need some of those big words when I go to college and or flying around the world in my corporate jet, as the CEO of my company.

Uncle Joe: Exactly! The main points I hope you take away from this conversation is:

1) There will always be "bullies." It doesn't matter what you do in life.

2) You have to learn how to handle bullies. What people say is either the truth or a lie. Liars lie.

3) Know who you are! The only one who has the right, authority, wisdom, and knowledge to tell you who you are is God.

4) Don't elevate people's definition of who they think you are above God's. They are not your creator.

5) Don't stay in the company or hang around those types of people. Some people stay near bullies or people who have those types of tendencies as though they have to have them in their life. If it is a family member and sometimes it is, as soon as you are able to remove yourself from their presence do so, so you can become who God has created you to be.

Any form of bullying can cause some people to harm themselves.

Brenda: You don't have to worry about me harming myself, but I might do harm to the bully though.

Uncle Joe: Yeah, I'm somewhat surprised that you are the one I'm having this conversation with, because you have a good sense of self.

Brenda: What do you mean?

Uncle Joe: During this bullying situation, what were you feeling?

Brenda: I was mad. People need to leave other people alone.

Uncle Joe: Did you consider changing your wardrobe or making any changes based on the things the "bully" said?

Brenda: No. I like what I have, how I dress, and who I am.

Uncle Joe: So, your self-esteem is intact.

Brenda: Yes.

SUICIDE

Uncle Joe: I'm glad to know that. There are some kids who are so consumed with what others think or say that they do harm to themselves. When I was teaching AFJROTC students, a part of the curriculum dealt with the subject of suicide. I was shocked to learn that suicide was the third leading cause of death for young people ages 14-24. I couldn't believe it. What's even more shocking is that it is now the second leading cause of death for that age group. I know of too many students who have ended their lives because of a person's words. When I first started teaching there was a student who was very talented, intelligent, and had a great personality. She also had a condition that caused her to have difficulty with her weight. I don't know if it was with her thyroid or what, but she was very sensitive about her size. She had dealt with this most of her life and as a senior in high school she was still struggling to come to grips with her condition. One day a student said something about her weight or size and she went home and ended her life.

Brenda: That's so sad.

BODY, SOUL, & SPIRIT

Uncle Joe: Yes, it is. She wasn't one of my students, but my heart still aches for the life that could have been. I wished I had had the opportunity to talk to her; to try to get her to see that there is more to us than just our physical body and that there are others who see beyond what you might deem to be unattractive.

Brenda: That sounds good, but you can't help seeing what you see.

Uncle Joe: Let me give you an example of what I mean. When I was in grade school, I had a teacher who I didn't find physically attractive until I got to know her as a person. She was caring, considerate, respectful, just a really nice lady. Her character and personality literally changed what I saw when I looked at her. As a young boy, she became attractive. I'm glad I learned this lesson early. People around the world uplift and promote physical beauty and that's not likely to change. We see it in most advertisements. Companies get the most physically attractive people to sell their products. A person with a certain size, shade, and look pulls us in because we've been conditioned to think that if I use this product, either I'll look like this person or people who look like this person will be attracted to me. It's psychological. They're using what we've been taught all our lives, "that physical beauty is most important," when in reality it's not. We, too often, believe that just because a person looks like an angel, that they are a good angel. The devil, Lucifer is one of the most beautiful and talented angels God created. Lucifer and a third of the angels in heaven got so caught up in his beauty and talent that they esteemed him greater than the one who created them all, and rebelled against God. These are beings who have been in God's presence for what could be millions or billions of years, yet they were swayed by what they saw.

Brenda: Okay...

Uncle Joe: On the flip side of that, there are people who are physically beautiful who don't think they are and go to extremes to become what they would describe as beautiful. They may take steroids, exercise excessively, have multiple plastic surgeries, don't eat right, all to the detriment of their health. The bible says, "As a man thinketh, so is he…" Our mind is a powerful instrument that can cause us to live in an unreality.

Brenda: Yeah, I know some people who are like that. There's this girl at school who is very pretty, but she doesn't think she is. She's always talking about her weight, hair, skin, different body parts and how she'd like them to be different. I told her, "girl if I had what you have I'd be thanking God," but it's like she can't hear me.

Uncle Joe: We need to realize that we are tripartite beings; body, spirit, and soul. The creation story, in the bible, says that God formed Adam out of the dust of the earth, breathed into him and he became a living soul. I heard a prominent pastor once put it this way, " We are a spirit, we have a soul, and we live in a body." I know a lot of people who over emphasize one of the three parts of their being above the others and lack balance in their lives.

Brenda: I understand the body part, but what do you mean when you say the soul and spirit are over emphasized?

Uncle Joe: So, let's say our soul is primarily our intellect. There are some people who are focused on intellectual pursuits. They don't eat right, exercise, or consider any spirituality. This person might be defined as a "bookworm," always seeking knowledge and neglecting everything else. They may even call themselves an atheist. Then you have those folks who are super spiritual where they are so involved in their spiritual endeavors, like praying, attending church all the time, attending bible study, only watching religious programming on television, and neglecting their body and soul. Having balance in life requires us to acknowledge all the parts of who we are and maintaining all aspects of who we are.

Brenda: That sounds like a lot of work.

Uncle Joe: I guess it depends on how you look at it. In my daily routine, I pray and read my bible which feeds my spirit man. I do some basic exercising and stretching every day, try to walk and or jog a few times a week, take vitamins and try to eat right to maintain my physical health and body. I read something every day and play games on my iPhone that are supposed to stimulate the mind or soul.

Brenda: Okay, I'm in school, so that's the soul part. I take PE and am involved in sports year-round, so that's the physical part and I read my bible at least once a week at church and pray before I eat my food and before I go to sleep at night.

Uncle Joe: Yeah, so you're working on all of who you are: soul, body, and spirit. You may want to increase the praying and bible reading parts though.

Brenda: Yeah...I kind of feel like I've been to church today.

Uncle Joe: I'll consider that as a compliment. Maybe I'll write this stuff down and put it in a book one day.

Brenda: You should. Thanks Uncle Joe.

JEALOUSY

Uncle Joe: What did you just say?

Niece (Cynthia): I said, "Tracy thinks she's so fine."

Uncle Joe: How do you know what Tracy thinks? Some of your aunts used to say that same thing. I've never liked hearing people make that statement.

Cynthia: I'm just saying the way she acts...I don't like it.

Uncle Joe: Could you be more specific?

Cynthia: She is always trying to get boys to pay attention to her.

Uncle Joe: What's wrong with that. You guys are teenagers. That's what girls and boys do at your age.

Cynthia: Well she needs to watch who she's trying to flirt with.

Uncle Joe: Why are you trying to be the flirt police?

Cynthia: Uncle Joe, with all due respect, why are you in my business?

Uncle Joe: Because I care about you and that statement, "She thinks she's so fine," reeks of jealousy.

Cynthia: I'm not jealous of her or anybody else.

Uncle Joe: So, you know I'm not passing judgement on you, but speaking from personal experience. When I was 19 or 20 years old I was jealous of a young man who I never took the opportunity to get to know. We were both stationed at an air force base in California and it appeared to me that he had personal qualities and things, like a nice car and clothes, that I did not possess. I was also in a relationship where trust was an issue, so I was emotionally unstable.

Cynthia: Emotionally unstable? What?

Uncle Joe: Yeah...I was trying to date this young lady who really wasn't that into me. I believe I was in love with her. This guy seemed to be the kind of guy she'd be attracted to. He didn't even know her. It was all in my head.

Cynthia: Yeah, that's being unstable, but what does this have to do with me?

Uncle Joe: Too often people spend a lifetime in a state of jealousy and envy, comparing themselves to others. When we stop looking at others to get a reflection of self and look to God to reveal our true reflection and embrace it, we find a sense of peace, joy, happiness, love, all that. I don't want you to get caught up in that state of mind and not focus on the gifts, talents, abilities, and purpose(s) God has gifted you.

Cynthia: Well, maybe I am a little jealous of her.

Uncle Joe: We just need to be honest with ourselves first. So, what's really going on with that, "She thinks she's so fine" statement?

Cynthia: Well, she is getting some attention from Cornell…

Uncle Joe: And…

Cynthia: I sort of like him.

Uncle Joe: Does Cornell know you like him?

Cynthia: I don't know.

Uncle Joe: He's Mr. Smith's son, right?

Cynthia: Yes.

Uncle Joe: From what I know of him, he's a nice young man. I'm not a match maker, but if you like him, get to know him. Befriend him. What do you have to lose?

Cynthia: But that's weird.

Uncle Joe: I'm not saying ask him to marry you or even date you, just be friendly and talk to him. You may find that he's really not your type or that he likes you too.

Cynthia: I'll think about it.

Uncle Joe: Like I said, I'm not a match maker. Let me put it like this, if your Aunt Ann hadn't shown interest in me, which resulted in our friendship, we would not have gotten married. I'm just saying...The main point is if there is jealousy present in you, be honest about it, check where it's coming from, and deal with it. Okay? Love you.

Cynthia: Love you too.

SEX

Uncle Joe: Tina and Rodney, your mom and I had a conversation a few days ago in reference to my having a conversation with you two.

Nephew (Rodney): Yeah, she talked to us about sex and wanted us to get a male's perspective, since our dad's not here.

Niece (Tina): You don't have to worry about me having sex and getting pregnant, because we watched films in sex education class where this lady was having a baby and I'm not going to go through all of that. I may just adopt a kid, if I decide I want to be a mom.

Uncle Joe: Well you may change your mind over the next few years after you meet your Romeo. Having sex doesn't always result in pregnancy, but I understand what you are saying. You both are about to turn 13 years old soon right?

Rodney: Yep, on the 29th. You know I'm older than her...

Tina: Yeah, only by about a minute.

Uncle Joe: Okay, so let's start this talk. I remember when I taught at a middle school many years ago. I was shocked at the conversations some of the students were having about their sexual exploits or experiences with each other without any concern about who may be listening. What shocked me most was that this girl was telling all her business. It really was concerning.

Tina: There are some girls who are nasty.

Uncle Joe: I don't mean to pass judgement in our talk, but you know I'm just real. You know that girl didn't just become "nasty." She was influenced by an adult. Adults mess kids up. We, adults, have to do a better job in raising our kids; like your mom and dad, before he passed away. Did you know that sex is God's idea?

Tina: I never really thought of it that way.

Rodney: Me either.

Uncle Joe: I'm sure you heard of Adam and Eve in the bible.

Tina & Rodney: Yes, in church and Sunday school.

Uncle Joe: In the book of Genesis it says that God created everything to include Adam and then He (God) saw that it wasn't good for man to be alone, so he put Adam to sleep, took one of his ribs and created a woman, who He called Eve. When Adam woke up he was like, "wow man!" He was very pleased with this creation.

Rodney: I bet Eve was "hot!"

Uncle Joe: No doubt she was fine, gorgeous, attractive, pretty, and any other word you can think of to describe her beauty.

Tina: Can we get back on the subject.

Uncle Joe: I'm sorry…

Rodney: You're just mad cause you don't look good.

Uncle Joe: Alright nephew, you know that's not true. Your sister is a pretty young lady…In the very near future you are going to have to be her bodyguard. Boys and young men will try to befriend you, just to get close to her.

Tina: Thank you Uncle Joe.

Uncle Joe: It's the truth.

Rodney: Can we get back on task Uncle Joe?

Uncle Joe: Like I was saying, sex is God's idea. After he made Eve, he told them to "be fruitful and multiply." In other words, have sex and make babies. Sex is good, righteous, wonderful in the confines of marriage. The problem is that with many things that God created, man has abused its purpose. Sex is meant to be enjoyed by a husband and his wife. Sex is great when it's done God's way. One of the major problems with sex is that it feels good whether you're married or not and people just want that good feeling. There is also pressure, even at your age, to have sex so that you are no longer classified as a virgin, or so you can "fit in." Even girls are often made to feel that something is wrong with them when they try to maintain their virginity. No one should ever be pressured into having sex before they are ready. Sex is not to be a rite of passage. Having sex with someone does not make you a man. A man is someone who is responsible for all

49

his actions. Waiting until you marry to have sex doesn't mean you are strange, it means you are strong. It means that you are a person who has standards, are disciplined, and have principles that you live by. As you probably learned in your sex education classes, there are possible consequences to having sex.

Tina: Yeah, you can get pregnant and have to raise the kid on your own.

Rodney: You can also get diseases.

Uncle Joe: And some of those sexually transmitted diseases (STDs) aren't curable. I had this talk with my kids, your cousins when they were about your age and through their teen years. I tried to make sure Nicole understood that when a female has a baby there is no guarantee the guy is going to stick around, so the risk for the female is great. It's not easy raising a kid with two parents. The difficulty is greatly increased when there is a single parent.

Rodney: Mom struggles sometimes.

Tina: Yeah, it can be hard at times.

Uncle Joe: I told your cousin Dias, if he got a girl pregnant he didn't necessarily have to marry her, but he was going to take care of the child, whatever that meant – getting a full-time job, joining the military or whatever. That kid didn't ask to be here and he or she deserves a mother and father. I wish I had had someone to talk to me the way I'm talking to you two. Neither one of your grandparents had the "sex talk" with me, so I didn't have any good opposition to what I was getting from television, my peers, and others. Your dad was a good man, who would have loved to have had this conversation with you two, if he had made it back from Afghanistan.

Rodney: We were little when he got killed so I don't remember much about him.

Uncle Joe: This conversation remains open, as far as I'm concerned, until you get married, so you can always call on your Uncle Joe, if need be.

Tina: Like I said earlier, I'm not having sex and risk having a baby so…

Uncle Joe: Okay, so let's go pickup your mom and Aunt Ann and get something to eat.

DATING

Tina: Uncle Joe, how old was Cousin Nicole when you let her start dating?

Mom (Sister): Why are you bothering your uncle about that?

Rodney: She didn't like your answer mom.

Tina: Nobody's talking to you blockhead.

Uncle Joe: Should I come back later?

Mom (Sister): No, I guess they didn't like my answer to the question.

Uncle Joe: I think Nicole was about 16. Why do you ask?

Tina: We were just talking about dating and what age is most appropriate to start dating.

Uncle Joe: I remember your Aunt Ann and I didn't agree on the age, but I'm pretty sure the youngest age for me was 16. I probably preferred her being 18. I dreaded the idea of Nicole dating. Fortunately, both Nicole and Dias were so busy working, dancing, playing sports, and school that they didn't do a lot of what I would call dating. They mostly went out with groups of kids. I know it's been a few years now, but I recall someone saying they weren't going to date, at least that's the impression I got.

Tina: If you are talking about when you talked to me and my brother about sex, that was a long time ago.

Uncle Joe: I'm sure I made mention of you having a change of heart someday.

Tina: Probably...Mom doesn't like the idea of me dating.

Mom (Sister): That's not true. I know it is inevitable. I just want you to be aware of some things and not be taken advantage of.

Uncle Joe: That was a scary time for me with Nicole. I was much more protective of her than I was with Dias.

Rodney: Well that's probably because Dias can't get pregnant.

51

Uncle Joe: You are probably right. Having been a knucklehead in my teens and early twenties I didn't know how to properly treat a young lady. I was listening to the wrong people and my motivations were less than pure. I was torn between my parent's rules and expectations and personal lustful expectations that would impress my friends and acquaintances. Your Aunt Ann taught me how to be a good date and a good man. She demanded it.

Tina: What do you mean?

Uncle Joe: Your aunt is a person of principles, standards, and expectations that she lives by, like your mom. When you date, as a young lady, you have to know what you will and will not do. For example, before I met your aunt I dated this young lady who wouldn't give me a kiss on our first date, not even on the cheek. That may have been our only date, as she told me later I had changed. We still remained friends though. It helps when a parent feels confident that their child, especially their daughter, won't be negatively influenced to do something they know they shouldn't do.

Tina: Like have sex.

Uncle Joe: Maybe not even kiss on the first date. Sex doesn't just happen. Usually kissing and touching (we'll call it) precedes the sexual act. As a father of a daughter and knowing how dumb I was, you need to know most boys or even young men aren't taught about relationships; that's not what is emphasized. Sex and how to get into a girls' panties is. Too many boys and young men see dating as a way to accomplish that goal. You just need to be aware of this fact. Our (me and your mom's) knowledge of this makes us hesitant about you dating. It's not so much a question of trusting you, but about your understanding of the mindset of some of the boys and young men in society. Unfortunately, I was one of them. This is why it's good that we're talking about this, so you aren't out there ignorant as to how, too many, young men think. It's good that you are hearing this too, nephew.

Rodney: Yeah, I guess so. I was talking to this girl and her mom must have thought I was trying to do what you just said, because she was rude to me, as though she knew me. She made accusations about my intentions and everything. The girl was telling her, he's not like that. He's just a friend, but she wasn't hearing any of that.

Uncle Joe: That reminds me of an incident I experienced when I was in high school. I didn't do much dating until I was grown, if you define dating as two people going out together. I didn't have any money to date before then. I do remember taking my friend's younger sister to a school dance. When I got to her house to pick her up her aunt was there and she was scary, on purpose, just like you described with your friend's mom. I started to turn around and just go back home. My date was apologetic about the interrogation I suffered through. She was a sweetheart of a person, so we went to the dance. We had a pretty good time. I got her home right after the dance was over, so as not to jeopardize my life. I'm pretty sure I didn't even try to kiss her. I didn't want her aunt to come after me. She was "gangster."

Tina: Okay, so back to the original question that I posed.

Uncle Joe: Like I said, Nicole was allowed to date at age 16, to answer your original question. Now you must understand that it's not like she could have just gone out with any guy, because she was 16. If some guy showed up at the house to pick her up and he had his pants hanging off his behind, looking unkempt, being disrespectful, or any of that, he would have left my house without my daughter. I then would have had a conversation with Nicole about what she was thinking. What made her think I would allow her to go out with someone who doesn't understand that he needs to make a positive impression before I'm going to let her go anywhere with him. Why didn't she prepare him for me and her mom? Did she tell him and he just ignored her? If so, then he disrespected her and her wishes and disqualified himself.

Tina: So, the guy has to meet your standards before you'd let him date Nicole?

Uncle Joe: Absolutely! Let me give you an example. If a guy is really interested in a young lady and he understands the dynamics of family structure. He's going to try to look and be his best. He understands that impressing the young lady's parents is very important. I'm not talking about superficial stuff. He's clean, respectful, and polite. Ultimately, I want my daughter and nieces to have a husband who is better than me or at least aspires to grow and be better.

Tina: Just because you are dating doesn't mean you're going to marry the guy.

Uncle Joe: That's true, but when you have the long-term relationship in mind you don't want to waste time with someone who, at the end of the day, has added nothing to you in word or deed. I heard it said that dating is literally gathering data about the person you are dating of course, but also about yourself. The few young ladies I "dated" before I met your aunt helped me see how much more she added to me. For example, this one young lady was very pretty and sweet, but when we talked we didn't communicate. We may as well have been speaking two different languages. I can't even begin to explain how frustrating that was. This other young lady didn't want what I wanted in life. I was in love with her, but our lives were headed in different directions. When I began "dating" your Aunt Ann her responses to the things I said were encouraging and rooted in wisdom and knowledge. Her goals in life were similar to mine and most importantly she laughed at my jokes.

Tina: Well you are funny sometimes.

Uncle Joe: It's just an innate gift from God.

Mom (Sister): My goodness. It must be time for you to go. I think I hear Ann calling you.

Uncle Joe: Before I go my dear sister, niece do you have any additional questions?

Tina: No, you have been very helpful.

Uncle Joe: Nephew, you have been pretty quiet over there.

Rodney: No Uncle Joe I'm good. All my ladies' parents love me.

Uncle Joe: Oh, so you got it like that huh?

Rodney: Yes Sir! I took notes from Cousin Dias. You remember that year he went to three proms.

Uncle Joe: Yes, I remember. One of those proms was at the school where I was working. I don't know where he got "it" from, but definitely not from me. Don't you get too big for your britches.

Rodney: I won't.

Uncle Joe: Alright sis, niece, and nephew...y'all be good.

Mom (Sister), Tina, Rodney: Bye-bye.

LIVE LIFE

Uncle Joe: Congratulations! You both graduated with some college credits under your belt.

Tina & Rodney: Thanks Uncle Joe.

Uncle Joe: It's been a while since we've talked and I wanted to speak to you two while I have the chance.

Rodney: No problem, what's up.

Uncle Joe: Over the years we've had some pretty heavy conversations about several things and I wanted to make sure you both know I'm always available, as long as I'm here on this earth. When your father didn't return from the Middle East I made it my business to try to "stand in the gap," with your mother's permission, and I'll continue to do that. Your experiencing the death of your father at an early age, may make this conversation easier for you to understand. You know that death comes at the end of life and we all must face it one day. We don't know when that day is, so I encourage you to live life. Don't just exist. Live life to the fullest. I say this, of course, because you guys are about to embark on your life's journey.

Rodney: This sounds like something from Star Trek.

Tina: Can you be serious for just one second?

Uncle Joe: No, that's okay. I want you two to always be who you are around me. I'm family and that's really what this conversation is about. Even though you are twins, you are two very distinct individuals.

Tina: Thank God for that!

Uncle Joe: See, I love it. I felt the love in that statement.

Rodney: I don't know Uncle Joe, that didn't sound like love to me.

Uncle Joe: It was love...but like I was saying you are individuals who have purpose and a destiny. Let your mission in life be to pursue who God made you to be. No one but God can tell you who you are. The way Christians hear from God is through reading the bible regularly, praying daily, and taking moments to be quiet to listen and meditate on God's word. I don't mean being spooky or weird, but improving your personal relationship with God, so you can hear His voice better. There will be plenty of people who will try to persuade you to do what they think you should do, for various reasons, but you need to know who you are so you can determine when other voices are just noise.

Tina: What do you mean by noise?

Uncle Joe: When I say noise, I mean like when the television is on in the background and you hear it, but you don't know what's being said because you aren't listening to it. You are concentrating on something else. There's no benefit to it nor are you distracted by it. You just hear it in the background. Now is the time when your childhood ends and your adulthood begins. I remember when your cousin Nicole left for military basic training, I cried like a baby.

Rodney: I've seen mom cry a few times lately. I don't like to see her cry.

Uncle Joe: I don't mean to be dramatic, because you know I don't like drama, but with Nicole I realized her childhood had ended; almost like a death. She would never be that little girl bouncing up and down, dancing around the house in a constant state of joy and glee. I was sad and proud at the same time. She had made an adult decision to do what was best for her at the time and she was following through with that decision. Your mom is having some of the same feelings with probably a greater depth of emotions because her life has been all about you guys. She, like good parents do, has sacrificed her wants and needs for her children. Even more so because she's had to do it without your father or any man to assist her.

Tina: I tried to get her to date Coach Jones, but she wasn't interested.

Rodney: I'm glad she didn't, that would have been weird. I do want her to be happy though.

Uncle Joe: Yeah...there are some fellows interested in dating your mom and now that you guys are leaving the nest she will probably consider moving on into that stage of life. She wanted to make sure she got you both to adulthood and she's done a great job. So now what about you? Now is the only time in your adult life that you have permission to be a little selfish.

Rodney: What, I get to be selfish?

Tina: You should be good at that.

Uncle Joe: Yes, a little selfish. You have to establish your likes, dislikes, personal standards and expectations. Your mom won't be there to stop you from going here and there and doing this or that. You will have to make those decisions for yourself. You are the captain of your ship. You determine your destination. It's wise for you to talk to your mom and other loved ones before making major decisions, but you are calling the shots. So, when I talk about being selfish I mean you really need to tap into who you are, who God made you to be and work on becoming...

Rodney: Well you know I'll have to make time for the ladies.

Uncle Joe: That's fine. I don't mean you have to be a hermit or a priest, but focused on your purpose – the reason you are here. You might even meet the person who will become your spouse. They should add to you, be encouraging, and a help in achieving your goals. If they are taking you away from what you are supposed to be doing they aren't what you need. In order to truly be happy in life you have to be fulfilled, knowing that you matter and that you make a difference. For me the greatest joy in life has been the reality that I have made a difference in the lives of people. I know I have made a difference in your lives and that gives me a sense of value that no one can take from me. It might be one small word or deed over the course of many years that may not be realized until you have children. I'm not trying to pat myself on the back, I'm being real.

Tina: Yeah Uncle Joe you've been there for us and mom a lot and we appreciate you.

Rodney: Yeah.

Uncle Joe: When you follow God's script for your life you are guaranteed to make a difference in the lives of others. He'll make sure you touch people's lives in ways that only you can. I plan on living to be a healthy old man, but if I were to die today, I can honestly say I've lived a great life. Everyday wasn't filled with joy and pleasantries, but it's been a blessed experience. I wasn't by any means perfect. I didn't always do the right thing, the right way, but I tried to make a positive difference in the lives of the people I came in contact with. So, this "selfish" period of your becoming whatever you are to become ultimately isn't for you, it's for everyone else. That's the bigger picture, if you would.

Rodney: That's kind of heavy.

Uncle Joe: It may sound that way, but it's just like how you arrived at today; living second by second, minute by minute, hour by hour, day by day and before you know it you are in the present. You can reflect back on approximately 18 years. I can reflect back on decades. You want the reflection to have been of value to others, with minimum regret. I'm proud of the young lady and young man you have become and believe you can achieve anything you set your heart and mind to. I believe we have a choice when it comes to our individual lives, as far as how we choose to live it.

Rodney: I don't know if I agree with that. There are some countries where if you are born poor you die poor.

Uncle Joe: That's true, but I'm talking about you, Americans of African descent. Life is meant to be lived to its fullest. This, no doubt, differs depending on an individual's personal likes and dislikes, but is still true. When I was a little kid I'd watch *Wild Kingdom* and other programs on television about animals in different places around the world and thought I'd like to be able to go there one day. I had this desire in me to travel and see the world. Honestly, that part of me is still alive and well. I love traveling, seeing different places, meeting different people and experiencing their cultures. That's one of the main reasons I joined the military after high school.

Rodney: If I have to join the military to see the world, I won't be seeing much of it.

Uncle Joe: Understood, but sometimes people never experience the fullness that life offers because they are constantly shooting ideas down. They come up with excuses to justify their hesitancy or even fear to do anything that will move them forward. A student may want a scholarship, but never takes the time to study or do homework. A person who says they always wanted to visit Europe or Africa, but complicates what is a simple matter…you need time and money and you can make the trip happen.

Rodney: Well I can see their point. When you went to Africa, how much was your plane ticket?

Uncle Joe: It was $3000, which included transportation, hotel, and meals. It was worth a lot more than that to me. Some things in life are priceless. The memories made will last a lifetime and there's no amount of money that can replace them. I just want to encourage you to be and do all that God has destined for you.

Tina & Rodney: Thanks Uncle Joe. We appreciate all you have done for us over the years.

Uncle Joe: It's been my pleasure. If you need anything I'm just a text away.

SEXUALITY

Nephew (Travis): Hey Uncle Joe.

Uncle Joe: What's up Travis?

Travis: Not much. What are you watching?

Uncle Joe: Nothing really. I'm just surfing through channels. What brings you to this part of town.

Travis: Mom is doing something with Aunt Ann, so I decided to drive her over and hangout with you for a minute.

Uncle Joe: Drive? I know they didn't give you a license.

Travis: Not yet. I have a permit. Why did you have to say it like that? I'm a great driver.

Uncle Joe: Yeah, I bet. Give me a call the next time you are driving, so I can make sure I'm at the house.

Travis: Ha-ha. Uncle Joe's got jokes.

Uncle Joe: I'm serious. I'm trying to live to be a healthy old man.

Travis: You are an old man.

Uncle Joe: I heard that.

Travis: Whoops!

Uncle Joe: You want something to eat or drink?

Travis: Sure, whatcha got?

Uncle Joe: I don't know, look in the fridge and help yourself. You probably need to drink some water. I know some young folks who never drink water.

Travis: I'm always drinking water. I learned about the importance of proper hydration in weightlifting class. Hey, Uncle Joe, can I ask you a personal question?

Uncle Joe: Sure, what's on your mind?

Travis: Okay, it's a hypothetical question.

Uncle Joe: Okay…what is it?

Travis: Well, if I was to tell you I'm gay, what would you say?

Uncle Joe: It depends on whether you mean you're happy or you are homosexual. If you mean you are happy, I would ask you why? If you mean you're homosexual, I'd ask you how do you know? In both cases I would ask for evidence.

Travis: I mean if I said I was homosexual.

Uncle Joe: How old are you?

Travis: I'll be 16 next month.

Uncle Joe: I'd really want to know why you think you are gay. I'd ask you some questions, not so much for my benefit, but for yours. You are the one who needs to be sure about something like that. Why are you talking to me about this?

Travis: Because you aren't fake. You'll tell me what you really believe and why. That's what I want to know.

Uncle Joe: Everyone doesn't consider that a positive quality.

Travis: Maybe not, but I do.

Uncle Joe: Okay then…I'd really ask you several questions…Especially in this case, when we're talking about a 15 or 16-year-old kid. I have never been physically or sexually attracted to another male. I love my male friends, but sex has never been a part of the equation for me. Sex, by the way, is the issue. For as long as I can remember I have always loved females and desired their touch and affection. There was a little girl in my neighborhood who I had a crush on my entire childhood. As a little kid sex wasn't on my mind, but I liked her in a way where being close to her was very special. If she had kissed me on the cheek, I would have been on cloud nine. I may have even passed out. Your telling me that you are gay wouldn't change my love for you. I truly would want to talk to you openly and honestly and see where the origins or beginnings of this thought lies. Then I would tell you what I believe about one's sexuality and why.

Travis: Like what?

Uncle Joe: Of course, you know I'm a Christian.

Travis: Yeah. So, you'll probably tell me I'm going to burn in hell.

Uncle Joe: No, that's not what I would say. I don't have a heaven or hell to put anyone in. I'm working hard enough to keep myself right with God. What I would say is, I believe all of what the bible says about everything. As smart as I may think I am, I can't pick and choose what to believe. The bible says that homosexuality is a sin, alongside lying, fornication, adultery, stealing, murder, and a host of other things. Homosexuality might not be an issue for me, but there are plenty of other sins that I have to contend with on a daily basis. Too often Christians are quick to get out of their place and judge a person on a sin that they don't have a problem with. God is our judge and the bible tells us not to judge one another. I'm thankful that God loves all his sinful children, even me and sent His son to pay the price for whatever our sins are. You didn't ask me to get a politically correct answer, did you?

Travis: No Sir. I was pretty sure you would tell me what you believe.

Uncle Joe: So, are you gay?

Travis: No, Uncle Joe.

Uncle Joe: Then why did you ask me that question?

Travis: Well, actually there's this girl who I really like. She's pretty, athletic, and smart, but she says she's gay.

Uncle Joe: Do you ever talk to her?

Travis: A little bit, but not the way I want to. It doesn't make sense to me that a fine girl like that should be with another girl. That's a waste.

Uncle Joe: How old is she?

Travis: 15.

Uncle Joe: That's what I don't understand...young people, teenagers and even pre-teens are claiming their sexuality before they know who they are. When I was your age there were very few teenage girls claiming to be lesbians. If I was you I wouldn't let her gay or lesbian title stop me from befriending her. The first thing is that I like her. The second is I'm curious about her psychology. Why do you call yourself gay? Do you want to know what I would tell her?

Travis: Sure!

Uncle Joe: After I got to know her a little bit better, I'd tell her that I really like you and I wish you weren't gay. You might want to word it differently. Question: Even if she says she's very gay and will always be gay, will that affect the way you feel about her?

Travis: Maybe eventually, but it will take some time. I really, really like this girl.

Uncle Joe: That's interesting. You know there are times when I questioned my sexual appeal.

Travis: What's that?

Uncle Joe: When I was a little younger than you, my voice was changing, hormones were raging, girls were developing and I questioned why girls weren't more interested in me. That caused me to question my manhood or masculinity. I was a skinny little kid. That phase may have lasted for a couple of years. Years later, when I was 21 or 22 years old, I was working out in the gym late at night and decided to take a shower before going back to the dorms. This is when I was in the Air Force. I was in the shower and I heard a noise, so I looked up and saw a guy getting ready to come in the shower. I had put some shampoo in my hair, yes, I had hair then, and noticed that I didn't hear another shower head turn on. I looked up again and this guy was standing beside me and said, "you have soap in your ear." We may have been the only two people in the gym. I immediately finished rinsing off, dried off, dressed, and left the gym. This was several years before you could be openly gay in the military. This incident messed me up. I questioned why this guy would approach me like that. Did I send him some kind of signal that made him think I was gay? To be honest I felt a little dirty. What are you laughing at?

Travis: You Uncle Joe. That's hilarious!

Uncle Joe: Yeah, it's funny now, but I was trippin before trippin was a word, then. I probably didn't shower for a week after that. I kept my clothes on 24/7.

Travis: You need to stop it, you really were trippin.

Uncle Joe: Yes, I was, but it's the truth: At least some of it. Our sexuality can be fragile. Some females cut their hair short and dress less femininely, because they have been sexually assaulted or abused. They feel safer when they believe they're viewed as less attractive to men. Some females may say they are gay or lesbian so they don't have to deal with guys, who too often have hurt them in the past. I believe there's always reasons for the way we think and act.

Travis: What if Nicole or Dias told you they were gay?

Uncle Joe: They're grown, so I would voice my personal concerns, but I wouldn't love them any less. I would be disappointed, but not so much in them, but in their decision. I believe we're supposed to live life, get married, for those who choose too, and have children. I know that's old school, but I'm old school.

Aunt Ann & Sister (Mom): Hey guys what have you two been up to.

Uncle Joe: We've been having an interesting conversation about sexuality.

Aunt Ann: What? Oh Lord...

Travis: Uncle Joe is funny.

Uncle Joe: It wasn't funny. Sis, you need to take your son back home.

Sister (Mom): Come on let's go.

Travis: See you later Uncle Joe and Aunt Ann.

Aunt Ann: Bye-bye.

Uncle Joe: You be safe driving my sister home.

Travis: Always.

DECISIONS

Uncle Joe: Darrell you only have a couple of years before you graduate high school, right?

Nephew (Darrell): Yes, and I can't wait.

Uncle Joe: So, it sounds like you are looking forward to life after childhood.

Darrell: Yes sir!

Uncle Joe: What are your plans?

Darrell: I'm going to go to college.

Uncle Joe: To pursue what?

Darrell: What do you mean?

Uncle Joe: What kind of degree are you going to pursue? What do you want to be after you complete your degree? A teacher, engineer, nurse…?

Darrell: I haven't decided yet.

Uncle Joe: What are you leaning towards?

Darrell: Well…to be honest I haven't really given that much thought yet.

Uncle Joe: There are some decisions that you are going to have to make now, so you can be ready for your future.

Darrell: I know, but there are so many decisions that have to be made.

Uncle Joe: Yeah, that's why you need to start making your plan, so you can work your plan. You have been making decisions as long as you have been alive, under the umbrella or covering of your parents. Now is the time you must start taking responsibility for the decisions you are about to make, because like you said, "I can't wait."

Darrell: What made you decide to join the Air Force after you graduated high school?

Uncle Joe: That decision was easy and very simple for me, unlike some others I have had to make over the years. My best friend's older brother was in the Air

Force and every time they'd talk about him he was in a different part of the world doing exciting things and that was what I knew, even at an early age, I wanted to be able to do. He went to college first, and became a commissioned officer, so that was how I was going to make it happen for me as well.

Darrell: But you didn't go to college right after high school…

Uncle Joe: No. Early summer, after graduation I was having a conversation with your grandmother and your mom in the kitchen and your mom said, "If I was you I would just go ahead and join now." That was the wisest thing your mom had ever said, to me.

Darrell: So, my mom helped you make that decision?

Uncle Joe: Yes. It made a lot of sense to me. The reason we were having the discussion was because I was complaining about having to attend the college right there in town. That college had Air Force ROTC and your grandfather wasn't going to pay extra money for room and board for me to go away for my schooling, which of course makes sense. I wanted to be independent and not live with my parents anymore, so the option of enlisting was the best thing for me to do.

Darrell: Yeah, that's how I feel, but I don't want to make any mistakes.

Uncle Joe: Well, I hate to be the one to tell you, but you are going to make some mistakes. You just want to minimize them in number and severity. Making mistakes is a human practice. It is what human beings do. That's not to give you a license to make "mistakes," or do anything you want and then call it a mistake. It's about realizing the importance of decision making, whether you consider the decision to be a minor or major one.

Darrell: Could you give me some examples of what you mean?

Uncle Joe: Sure, I can give you a lot of examples. In this state it's legal to smoke marijuana. I'm old enough to do it, but is it something I should do? When I was about your age I decided I no longer wanted to be a virgin, so I had sex with a girl who was willing so I could say "I'm not a virgin."

Darrell: Uncle Joe, I don't want to know all of that.

Uncle Joe: Maybe you don't, but that was a really bad decision. That decision was made for totally selfish reasons. It could have drastically changed both of our lives. I was only concerned about one thing and that was about changing my virginity status. I wish I had been more mature and self-confident, but that was how I was then, trying to live up to the expectations of my peers. If she had gotten pregnant my peers would not have had any responsibility, just me. The decisions we make in life determine our destination. Decisions are like the rudder to a ship or a steering wheel to a car that we, and we alone, are in charge of. You can listen to as many voices as you want to, as far as which direction to turn, but you are the one who is responsible for where you end up.

Darrell: Okay, I get it, but...

Uncle Joe: I know people, even family, don't talk about their personal real-life issues and experiences and I think generations are hurt because of our hesitance to do so. I told that story to your cousin, Nicole.

Darrell: You did. What did she say?

Uncle Joe: "Ooh daddy." The way she said it was like that's terrible. How could you have done such a thing? I wanted her to understand that even "good guys," as she might interpret me as being, make bad decisions at times and we all need others to help guide us towards more positive decisions and behavior.

Darrell: You two seem to have a really good relationship.

Uncle Joe: Yes, we do. I'm grateful for it. So back to some of the other decisions I made and how I came about them. When I was in basic training I filled out my "dream sheet," a form you fill out to have the possible opportunity to go to various locations around the world. I put down California, to impress my friends back home and because I had envisioned fine ladies on the pacific coast beaches. While I was stationed in California, a few years before I met your Aunt Ann, I was talking to an older sergeant who was telling me about England and all that he had done and the fun experiences he had while he was stationed there. A few days later I changed my "dream sheet," and in a couple of months I had an assignment to England. Near the end of my time in England I met your Aunt Ann. We became close friends in a very short period of time and a little over a year later we got married. Getting married to your Aunt Ann was probably the scariest and yet rewarding decision I have ever made. I really didn't want to make a mistake and ruin either of our lives. One day I'll tell you more about how hard I was trippin.

Darrell: Yeah, I'd want to hear more about that because me and Susie are pretty tight.

Uncle Joe: Boy, what are you, 16 years old?

Darrell: Yeah, but you know…

Uncle Joe: Yes, I know…another decision made was when I decided to change career fields and become a recruiter. I had been somewhat interested in recruiting since I talked to my recruiter during my initial processing into the Air Force, years earlier. It seemed like a good job, with some additional benefits so I applied and got it. I had been taking some classes without declaring a major over the first five or so years I was in the Air Force and decided to pursue Human Resources. It aligned with recruiting and I thought it would be the best major for me at the time. My goal or plan was to at least have a baccalaureate degree before I retired, which I was able to accomplish. I almost got out of the Air Force around my eleventh year because I hadn't made rank in six years. I had signed my early release paperwork and everything, but I really wasn't prepared to get out. I didn't have a solid plan of what I was going to do. I had made a bad decision.

Darrell: What did you do?

Uncle Joe: Fortunately, I made rank and was given the option to stay in, which I took without hesitation. God helped this brother out. I'm so glad I was able to stay in and retire.

Darrell: You get a check every month, right?

Uncle Joe: Yes, I do and it's made a huge difference in my family's socio-economic status. I could go on and on about the thousands upon thousands of decisions I have made over the years, but I'll leave you with these two. After I retired from the military I began teaching in the public-school system. I did that for about five years and was encouraged to apply for this Principal Fellows

Program sponsored by the state to develop school principals. Now I never thought I would ever get a scholarship. A fellowship is much better than a scholarship because I was literally paid to complete a master's degree in school administration. I was a full-time student for two years.

Darrell: Mom has always said you were smart.

Uncle Joe: Well, that's nice that she thinks so, but what I found out is it's so important that I have some sense of believing that about myself. My being able to qualify to apply for the fellowship is a result of multiple decisions made on a daily basis. I had to have a certain GPA, which meant I had to take classes, study, do my homework, read stuff I cared nothing about, while working a full-time job and make A's and B's. If I had not done these things and more, the fellowship would not have been an option for me.

Darrell: It sounds like a lot of work.

Uncle Joe: Yes, becoming what one might characterize as successful requires work. Making the decision is the beginning or foundation, then comes the work. So, it's helpful to make good decisions consistently if you want to achieve anything of value in life. It is likely that you'll make some bad decisions as well, but don't let them keep you down. Apologize, ask for forgiveness or whatever you can do to make it right. Learn from it and keep it moving. Lastly, what I believe is the most important decision everyone must make deals with the part of our being that too many neglect.

Darrell: What's that?

Uncle Joe: Our spiritual being. We are body, soul, and spirit. We know that death is the final destination for all of us, but is that the end of our existence? The part of us that is most like God is our spirit. I believe the soul and spirit of our being are eternal. It's important that we accept the gift of salvation, made possible through the work of our Lord and Savior Jesus Christ. That's the most important decision we all must make. Have you made that decision?

Darrell: Yes Sir, a few years ago, but I don't always do the right thing.

Uncle Joe: None of us do. It is a consequence of our humanity. So, start working on and defining your future plans. If you need any help or assistance let me know and I'll do what I can.

Darrell: Thanks!

WAYWARD CHILD

Uncle Joe: Hey Tommy, weren't you supposed to be with your mom when she came to pick me up from the airport?

Nephew (Tommy): I don't know.

Mom (Sister): Yes, you do, you better stop lying boy!

Uncle Joe: Where were you and why didn't you do what your mom asked you to do?

Tommy: I didn't want to go.

Mom (Sister): And, where were you?

Tommy: With some of my friends.

Uncle Joe: Do your friends wear a flag hanging out of their back pocket and have their pants sag below your waist like you?

Tommy: What's up with all these questions?

Uncle Joe: All these questions are about how you have been behaving over the past several months: Disrespecting your mom, doing what you want to do when you want to do it, hanging out with gang members, getting in trouble at school. That's what's up with all these questions. Your mom and I talked and I decided I'd come down and talk to you. I didn't want to believe the things she was telling me.

Tommy: That's what's wrong with this family, people are always telling other people about my business.

Mom (Sister): Boy you're 14 years old, you don't have any business.

Uncle Joe: And we're family. What you do is my business.

Tommy: You're my uncle, not my daddy.

Uncle Joe: I know I'm not your daddy. He's in jail and it appears that you are trying to join him. What happened to the nephew I spoke to the last time we met?

Tommy: He's dead.

Mom (Sister): He's dead! I can't sit here and listen to this foolishness. (Mom goes to her room as she starts to cry.)

Uncle Joe: Tommy, what happened to you? You've known me all of your life and I thought we were cool.

Tommy: I guess you thought wrong.

Uncle Joe: Wow. I have seen this before when I was working in the school system and I don't like what I'm seeing. It is obvious that you are involved with a gang. It doesn't take a genius to see that. If it looks like a duck, walks like a duck, quacks like a duck, it's a duck. The reason I'm here is because your mom, my sister, shared somethings with me about your behavior over the past several months and I told her I'd come down and talk to you.

Tommy: You could have saved your time and money…

Uncle Joe: Yeah, I could have, but this is what love looks like. I love my sister, your dad, and you. I wanted to at least try to talk to you and even have you come stay with me and your Aunt Ann for as long as needed, if you wanted to get out of the gang or just get away.

Tommy: Nah, I'm not going anywhere.

Uncle Joe: Okay. You are 14 years old, which means to me that you are old enough and smart enough to make that decision. I'm old enough and wise enough to know that you can't stay in my house for a minute if you are going to be disrespectful, because you'd see a side of your uncle that I don't even want to see.

Tommy: I'm not scared of you.

Uncle Joe: I know you aren't. I'm scared of what might happen, if I don't use the good sense God gave me. I don't do well with "stank attitude" children. So, let me say what I came to say and you won't have to hear anything else from me. When I was about your age I had a terrible argument with my mom, your grandmother. I said some stupid things and upset her to an extent I didn't know I could. A day or so later your grandad sat me down and told me something that I really didn't understand before the conversation. He told me how much my mom, your grandmother loved me and many of the things she had done for me. I wasn't as "hard" as you so I began to cry like a baby. From that day until mom died I promised myself that I'd never cause her any more harm or pain, in any way. That was a decision I made and kept. I didn't share it with anyone, not even your grandma.

Tommy: Why are you telling me this story?

Uncle Joe: The reason I'm telling you this is because this is a very similar scenario. You are hurting your mother. The reason she left and went into her room is because she's hurting because of you. Children don't understand the power they have over their parents and the depth of love their parents have for them. Your mom has lost your dad for a number of years, because he's locked up. Now she's losing you. Her only child. I don't know if you love your mother, but I loved your grandmother. She was my everything. I'm a momma's boy and proud of it. Your mother hasn't done anything to deserve being treated the way you're treating her. She's working two jobs to keep food on the table, clothes on your back, and a roof over your head. After this conversation, you are going to have to decide as to how you are going to respond. The life of a gangster or thug is not enjoyable. The risk of imprisonment, suffering physical and or mental harm, and even death is real. All you have to do is look around you. You don't have to be a statistic, but you can choose to be one and there's nothing any one of us who love you can do about it. The decision you make after this conversation will determine the direction your life will take. I'm telling you what I know to be true. I'm not going to say anything else to you during my brief stay, unless you ask me something. The ball, as they say, is in your court. What are you going to do with it? I'm going to check on your mom.

(THREE YEARS LATER)

Uncle Joe: Hey nephew.

Tommy: Hey Uncle Joe.

Uncle Joe: Your mom told you I'd be picking you up, right?

Tommy: Yeah, she said she had a lot going on and she wanted to have my favorite meal ready when I got back. I know she doesn't like long rides in the car either.

Uncle Joe: I haven't seen you in a few years and I don't mind a couple hours' drive every now and then, plus I get to spend some quality time with my nephew. So, you holding up alright?

Tommy: Yeah, I'm good. I'm happy to be out of this place.

Uncle Joe: I can only imagine.

Tommy: It wasn't hell, but two years of my life was spent here and I missed out on too many things.

Uncle Joe: What kind of things?

Tommy: Girls, parties, freedoms to go and do what I want to do, family, all of that...

Uncle Joe: But you know what, your time in there may have saved your life.

Tommy: Yeah, I thought about that. Mr. Carl, my counselor, told me about his thug life before he turned his life around and he was saying how many of the guys he used to hang with are dead or in prison. He was really the one who helped me see that I needed to make a change.

Uncle Joe: Your mom told me how well you have been doing with your grades, behavior, and attitude.

Tommy: Yeah, like I said in talking to Mr. Carl and just looking at how this situation went down. None of the fellows I was hanging with wrote me, called me, or even tried to contact me through mom. All of that opened my eyes to the fact that I had to decide what I want in life and this crap ain't it.

Uncle Joe: This is the nephew I know. We all go through things and how we respond to them can vary from one extreme to another. The important thing is that we come to ourselves before it's too late. Remember the story I told you about the argument I had with your grandmother when I was about 14 years old?

Tommy: Yeah.

Uncle Joe: It only took a conversation with your grandad for me to make a change. Sometimes it takes a more severe jolt in life for us to come around. Unfortunately, there are times when the person never changes or at least not in time to avoid terrible consequences.

Tommy: When we talked last I wasn't ready to hear anybody. I was so mad at everybody, even mom. My dad was in jail and I blamed him, mom, and myself. There was nothing I could do to change the situation, so I rebelled. There was nothing anyone could have said that I would have heard then. I wasn't listening.

Uncle Joe: That's what I thought and felt. That's why I just left you alone. I prayed for you, but I didn't think I would be the one to speak what you needed to hear, the way you needed to hear it. It sounds like Mr. Carl is the one God used to reach you.

Tommy: Yeah, it's something about how he spoke to us. I saw myself in him and the stories about his experiences. I guess God did use him.

Uncle Joe: I'm just glad to have my nephew back.

Tommy: I'm glad to be back.

Uncle Joe: Have you communicated with your dad recently?

Tommy: I got a letter from him about a week or so ago. He was excited that I was about to get out. He should be out in about a year from now.

Uncle Joe: Maybe he'll be able to see you graduate.

Tommy: That would be nice.

Uncle Joe: I know he'll be proud of you.

Tommy: Yeah, he wasn't happy with me at all when I got sent away, but it wasn't much he could say, since he's in jail himself.

Uncle Joe: Yeah, there's some truth to that, but every parent, who cares, wants their children to do better than them.

Tommy: That makes sense.

Uncle Joe: If you think you will have a difficult time in going back to your old neighborhood, you can come and stay with me and your Aunt Ann. We've talked about it with your mom and you are welcome to complete your last year of school with us: But just like our kids, once you graduate you've got to go; be it college, military, or joining the workforce.

Tommy: We'll see. I don't think I'll have a problem. I really would like to stay with mom and try to make up for the misery I have caused her. She's worked hard trying to raise me in the right way and I've been a bum.

Uncle Joe: What are you planning on doing after you graduate?

Tommy: I'll probably go in the military. I know you did and Mr. Carl was in the Marines.

Uncle Joe: That sounds like a good idea. What about me and Mr. Carl's being in the military moved you to consider it.

Tommy: Well, I don't want to be a burden to mom financially and I know I'll need some skill or level of education beyond high school to make decent money, so the military looks like the best option for me.

Uncle Joe: You sound like me when I made the decision to go in the Air Force. I wanted to be independent of my parents, be able to continue my education, to travel and see the world.

Tommy: Exactly. That's what I want.

Uncle Joe: If you have any questions about the Air Force and or the process of enlisting don't hesitate to ask me. I was a recruiter for most of the time I was in. Well we're here. I'll wait in the car for a few minutes to let you and your mom have a moment. I may give your Aunt Ann a call before I come in.

Tommy: Okay. How long are you going to be in town?

Uncle Joe: I may be leaving sometime late tomorrow.

Tommy: Okay, we can talk later. Thanks Uncle Joe.

Uncle Joe: My pleasure.

(A FEW HOURS LATER)

Uncle Joe: So how does it feel to be home?

Tommy: Great! I haven't been this happy in a long time. It feels like it did when I was a young kid, before I started trippin. I just wish things had been different with our family.

FAMILY

Uncle Joe: Let me tell you a little about your grandparents and my experience growing up. You may be aware of most of what I share through your mom, but even though we grew up in the same household our individual perspectives may be different. I was the third child, first male born of what would be a total of six children. Your grandfather was a Baptist pastor of two churches in small communities in North Carolina. He worked out of state as an English teacher for most of my childhood. Your grandmother was a housewife, who would do a few lady's hair and clean and cook for a select few well-to-do folks in the area. Both your grandparents were selfless people; always doing for others, before self. We were not a touchy-feely kind of family. There were very few hugs and kisses given, though I love it when dad would occasionally give mom a kiss on the lips in our presence. It gave me a sense of comfort, confirming that their relationship was intact. The first time I remember ever hugging my dad was when I was an adult. Either I was on my way to California for the first time or returning after taking a few days of leave. I was in the Air Force at the time. I remember once hugging my mom, as a kid, sitting on the edge of my bed, trying to console her as she cried because, at least on the surface, the water heater was acting up and dad was trying to fix it. I'm sure it was more to her emotional display than that, but I was unaware of what it was. It was obvious to me that dad was the leader of the family. Your grandparents may have had private counsel before decisions were made, but dad had the final say. Your grandma was the disciplinarian. She wore a leather belt out on my little, knucklehead, hind parts. I was sandwiched between two sets of older and younger sisters. Your Uncle Van was the last one to arrive. I was glad to finally have a brother, but he was too young to balance the female majority, and though dad had the final say in major things he was oftentimes absent, because of work or church matters, to cast his vote. I was blessed to have a wonderful neighbor with a son my age and one two-years younger, who allowed me to spend a lot of time with them. Because of your grandfather's work schedule my relationship with him was distant. If I wanted to be in his physical presence, my best bet was to be in church. When he was home he spent much of his time in his home office reading, resting, praying, studying and communicating with his congregation. Unfortunately, there are only 24 hours in a day and very little of that time was family time. This was difficult for me as a son who loved, respected, and admired his father, but could not freely converse with him. Your grandmother, on the other hand, was present to converse with. I learned that the best time to do so was in the kitchen, while helping her prepare dinner. I could ask her questions about her childhood and she'd tell me stories that gave me some insight as to who she was as a person. I longed to do the same with dad, but opportunities were hard to find. Your grandmother passed away at the age of 60. She had given all she had to her family. She had always said she wanted to live long enough to see her children grow up. I wish she had asked God for more, but that's the kind of person she was; humble, caring, worried about too much, and was selfless. Your grandad passed away about 12 years after mom. Our relationship was the best it had ever been before his passing. God had granted us another chance to have the kind of relationship I had longed for as a child and I am grateful for that. A few months before his death, he sat down with me and your Aunt Ann and complimented us on the way we were raising our children, his grandchildren and said how proud he was of us and how much he loved us. I had no idea he'd be gone three months later. That conversation with my dad was like a medicine for me and I believe it was a sort of emotional healing for him as well.

Family is very important. It's where our first relationships are formed. Mother births the child, holds him close, and feeds him from her own body. Ideally dad is present and assists in his development. If he has older siblings he's quickly introduced to them. His existence and identity are framed by these human beings who are literally closest to him. But what happens when he doesn't have a loving mother, or dad can't be found or is abusive? This child's view of family will probably be damaged because of the dysfunction in which he finds himself.

Tommy: My family is definitely dysfunctional.

Uncle Joe: So are many others. Family dysfunction isn't limited to certain folks. Every race, ethnicity, socioeconomic level (rich or poor), Christian, heathen, you name it, experiences some level of dysfunction. My family as a child and as an adult has suffered some level of dysfunction, if for no other reason, because I am a part of the family. I'm not saying this because I believe I am a bad person. I believe dysfunction exists because we all have our shortcomings. The bible says we all have sinned and come short of God's glory. There are a multitude of levels of dysfunction, caused by a variety of circumstances. A single parent, drug abuse, neglectful or abusive parents, or a wayward child. I'll never forget this, we were having a family meeting, of sorts, where we were saying things we liked and disliked about each other, and we were to be open and honest. It came time for Dias to say what he thought about me. I forget what he said he liked about me, because what he said he disliked was the last thing I wanted to hear. He said, "sometimes you are mean." He was probably 11 or 12 years old at the time. Those words went straight to my heart. That is not what I want my kids to think about me. Even though this was the same child who would tell his mother she was being mean when he was younger and he couldn't have his way, but this was different. Admittedly, I was stricter with him than I was with his sister. Negative words or raising my voice in anger affected him more than they did his sister, so from that day on I have tried to do better and be better in that regard. I don't want that to be what he remembers about me. Once, I had asked my dad, your grandfather, about his father and he said, "All I can remember about him is that he was bald, yellow, and mean." This is the memory that was burned in the mind of a five-year-old child. His dad died when he was five. You were born to my sister and your dad. You didn't have any say in the matter. You responded to the dysfunction in your family in a way that caused you to be locked up for a couple of years. That is your history, you don't have to let it be your legacy.

Tommy: I know, but I feel bad about all the stuff I did, especially how I disrespected and hurt my mom.

Uncle Joe: No doubt...that shows that you have a heart. You have been given another chance in life to become whatever you choose to be. Have you asked God for forgiveness?

Tommy: Yes. Several times.

Uncle Joe: Then He has forgiven you. Now you need to forgive yourself for the things you've done, as difficult as that may be, and move forward – looking forward. You can't help but to remember the past, but live in the present, and plan for your future. Become the man you choose to be. You seem to admire Mr. Carl.

Tommy: Yeah, a lot.

Uncle Joe: Well, that's a good place to start. As you grow and become, aspire to be the "Mr. Carl" to other young people, making a positive impact in their lives like he has yours. I think those actions will help you to heal and forgive yourself as well.

Tommy: Thanks Uncle Joe. I appreciate you coming and picking me up and being there for me.

Uncle Joe: I'm your family, that's what I'm supposed to do. I'm going to bed now. That drive wore me out.

Tommy: I'll be cooking breakfast in the morning. Is there anything special you'd like?

Uncle Joe: Where did you learn to cook?

Tommy: When I was locked up I started cooking. Everybody says I'm pretty good at it.

Uncle Joe: Well I guess I'll see tomorrow morning. Whatever you cook I'll eat. Cook what you consider to be your best meal, with the exception of oatmeal. I don't do oatmeal. That's some slimy stuff.

Tommy: Okay. Good night.

FOLLOW-THROUGH

Tommy: Thanks for coming with mom and dad to my basic training graduation.

Uncle Joe: I wouldn't have missed it. I sort of feel like I recruited you. So far do you think you made the right decision to join the military?

Tommy: Yes, it was either the Marines or Air Force and I think the Air Force is more compatible with what I want to get out of my military service experience.

Uncle Joe: I know your dad was super excited and proud of you and being able to come down to witness the ceremonies.

Tommy: Yeah. He wasn't able to come to my high school graduation because he got out of jail a couple of months later. This makes up for that. He and mom seem to be happy.

Uncle Joe: Yes, they do. Your dad was able to get a job in construction and I believe he's a new man, so don't you worry about them.

Tommy: I won't. I'll be busy keeping myself straight.

Uncle Joe: I know your parents are very proud of you. You made a plan when you were released from lockup and followed through with what you said you'd do: Helped your mom around the house, worked part-time, graduated from high school, enlisted in the military, and have graduated from basic training. I want to encourage you to continue to make your plans to achieve your goals and then work your plan.

Tommy: I am. When I get to my first duty station, as soon as I can, I'm going to start taking college courses.

Uncle Joe: Excellent! You may become an officer. Maybe even a General.

Tommy: I don't know about all that, but thanks for believing in me.

Uncle Joe: You can be whatever you want to be, never forget that. Not because I say so, but because God says so. I'm going to leave you with that. I'm driving up to visit your cousin, Dias.

Tommy: Oh yeah, he and his wife do live in Texas. Maybe I'll get stationed at the same base someday.

Uncle Joe: It could happen. If you need anything don't hesitate to call, text, or message me.

Tommy: I will. Thanks again for coming. It means a lot to me.

Uncle Joe: My pleasure. You know you've always been my favorite nephew.

Tommy: Yeah, right...See you later Uncle Joe.

Uncle Joe: Bye, Airman...Tommy.

READING

Uncle Joe: Hey nephew. Did you come out here to help me fix your mother's car?

Nephew (Ricky): Not really...It was either come out here to help you or read a book or something.

Uncle Joe: Either way you'll have an opportunity to learn something.

Ricky: But it's summer break. I'm not in school right now.

Uncle Joe: No, you're not in the school building nor are you going to get a grade, per se, for reading or being out here with me, but learning something is a possibility.

Ricky: I guess, but reading is boring.

Uncle Joe: It can be if you are reading about things you don't care about. What are you interested in?

Ricky: What do you mean?

Uncle Joe: Do you like cars, traveling, animals?

Ricky: I like sports. I know stats about most of the best players in basketball, football, and soccer.

Uncle Joe: How much do you know about the history of those sports?

Ricky: Not much.

Uncle Joe: Knowing when, where, and how those games were developed may be interesting to know.

Ricky: Yeah, maybe.

Uncle Joe: If I bought you a book like that would you read it?

Ricky: Yeah, I think so.

Uncle Joe: When I was a kid I didn't like to read either. My thinking was like yours. Your grandad had all kinds of books in his office. He had the classics like

Moby Dick and Tom Sawyer. Those are the only ones I can remember, because like I said, I didn't read them.

Ricky: How many books did he have and why?

Uncle Joe: He probably had 200 or so, that he used when he was a high school English teacher. Your grandad was kind of funny about his book collection. I think he thought we'd tear them up. He probably was right and I didn't care because I didn't want to read them anyway. When I became an adult and had children I began to understand the importance of reading.

Ricky: What do you mean?

Uncle Joe: Something happens to the brain when we read that makes us better learners or we learn while we're reading. If nothing else our reading helps to improve our vocabulary. We may come across words that we don't know, look them up in the dictionary or get an understanding of what the word means by the way it's used in the text. When I was a recruiter in the Air Force one of our recruiting requirements had to do with helping high school students with their ROTC scholarship applications. The applicants had to have a certain GPA and SAT or ACT score to qualify.

Ricky: What's a GPA, SAT or ACT?

Uncle Joe: GPA is an acronym that stands for grade point average. You'll learn more about that when you get to high school. Just make A's and B's and you'll have a good GPA. SAT and ACT are also acronyms. I forget what each letter represents, but they are tests you take to qualify for entrance into most colleges and universities. I did an informal survey of the ROTC scholarship applicants, asking what they attributed their intelligence to? Every one of them said reading was one of the major attributing factors. They read books, magazines, newspapers or whatever they could regularly. If I had read just a little bit, compared to not at all, I probably would have qualified for an academic scholarship to attend college.

Ricky: Yeah, right.

Uncle Joe: No, I'm serious.

Ricky: No, I was talking about me. You have a master's degree and all of that.

Uncle Joe: Yes, I was able to continue my education while I was in the Air Force and did well, but I would have had the option to go to a college at least an hour or so away from my parent's house...maybe even out of state. Reading may provide you with options that you never thought you would have. I'm telling you what I know.

Ricky: Well, maybe I'll go back in the house and see if I can find a book to read.

Uncle Joe: No, you are out here now. You are going to help me with this brake job. It won't take long. You'll learn something and then have time to read a little later, since you're on summer break.

Ricky: Come on Uncle Joe.

Uncle Joe: You need to know this too. The next time it needs to be done, you'll know how to do it and maybe I'll just supervise.

Ricky: Yeah, right.

Uncle Joe: Maybe later this week we'll go to the library or book store and look for some books on the sports that you like.

Ricky: None of it seems like fun to me, but...

Uncle Joe: A few years from now you'll be grateful for both this conversation and the automotive "training."

Ricky: We'll see.

Uncle Joe: Yes, we will. Now pass me that ratchet.

PROFANITY

Ann: Hi Honey, I'm home.

Uncle Joe: How was your day?

Ann: Nothing out of the ordinary, really.

Uncle Joe: That's good.

Ann: I am working with a teacher who is upset because she has a student who cusses "all the time."

Uncle Joe: What grade is the kid in?

Ann: First.

Uncle Joe: I remember when I was in the first grade, there was a kid in the class that cussed like a sailor. Every other word was profanity. Most of the kids thought it was funny; myself included.

Ann: Well, this teacher doesn't find it funny at all. I'll talk to our counselor tomorrow to get her to assist her and the student.

Uncle Joe: That sounds like a good idea. There was this other kid, when I was in high school who cussed all the time too. I remember thinking, dude you cuss so much that what you're saying doesn't even make sense. His use of profanity was more than every other word. As a teenager I thought him less intelligent and I wasn't too bright myself. When I started teaching I found that a lot of kids cussed without any respect to adults being present. It's just the way some of them talk. I came to understand that this is their language.

Ann: It may be their language, but they need to learn to switch it up, per their audience or change it altogether. There's no excuse for a teenager speaking like that. That's so disrespectful. If Nicole and Dias had tried that…

Uncle Joe: You remember that time Nicole said, "dammit," at school?

Ann: Yes, she was in the first grade. The teacher called me immediately and I went up to the school and dealt with it.

Uncle Joe: I played along with the act of being upset and disappointed with her, but I have to admit, I thought it was funny. I knew she was imitating someone she had observed outside our household and that the teacher's and your quick response would clearly inform her that using that word was a no-no.

Ann: That's why we need to have the support of parents. We have to work together for the child's sake.

Uncle Joe: No doubt. We have to help the student learn that although profanity may be used in the way they speak at home and in their neighborhood, in most other places it is deemed unacceptable. If we equate it as another language, in the literal sense, and understand that this is the language used in their home, we can better help the child, in their early years.

Ann: What do you mean?

Uncle Joe: For example, when a Spanish speaking student comes to school we encourage them to speak English, because it is the dominant language of our country and culture. Their parents may speak little or no English at all. In order for the student to properly acclimate into society they are taught proper English. The student who uses a lot of profanity should be treated similarly in that he needs to be taught proper English as well. Teachers may need to get some training in this concept of profanity being a language to change their approach to the issue, and try not be offended by the students who speak this way. They are just using the language that they have been taught. These kids are a product of their environment. Everyone wasn't raised in a home like mine where we knew not to cuss. We knew the consequences would have been severe. In some other homes, literally everybody uses those words all the time. It's going to take some time and patience to help those kids get beyond where they are.

Ann: It would be a lot better if all of our parents would work with us.

Uncle Joe: Yep. That's why pre-schooling, from birth to kindergarten, is so important. All we can do is keep hope alive and do what we can, wherever we find ourselves. What I tried to do when I was in the school system was to establish a rapport with kids, so I could speak to those types of issues. When a student used profanity, I might say "language" and hear sorry Mr. Peek, acknowledging the error made. The student knew the correction I was requesting was for their good; my wanting them to be their best, for their benefit. I know you do that kind of thing as well. I'm preaching to the choir.

Ann: The saying "people don't care how much you know, until they know how much you care," is true.

Uncle Joe: Maybe I can start mentoring some students at your school, in my spare time.

Ann: So, you'll be at school on a daily basis?

Uncle Joe: That sounds awfully shady. No, I'll have to check my schedule and see where I can fit that in.

Ann: Please do. What are we having for dinner?

Uncle Joe: Whatever you'd like. You know I don't cook on Tuesdays.

Ann: It's Thursday.

WORK

Nephew (Kevin): Uncle Joe, how old were you when you got your first job?

Uncle Joe: My first real job...when I was 16. Why do you ask?

Kevin: Mom and dad are telling me it's time for me to start looking for a job.

Uncle Joe: How old are you now?

Kevin: 15.

Uncle Joe: Well, like I said I was 16 when I started working at a restaurant, bussing tables and washing dishes. I call it my first real job because that's when I learned about taxes.

Kevin: Taxes?

Uncle Joe: Yes, taxes. I had worked for two weeks and had calculated my hours and whatever I was supposed to make per hour. I think minimum wage was less than three dollars then.

Kevin: That must have been back in the 1950s or something.

Uncle Joe: No, it was in the 1970s...Anyway, the dollar amount on my check was a lot less than what I had calculated. I was upset about that thing. I thought they had made a mistake, until it was explained to me what FICA is.

Kevin: What's that?

Uncle Joe: Taxes, federal tax. There probably were other taxes as well. To this day, I don't believe the government should tax a person's wages. Before I had this job, on rare occasions I would cut people's grass and do a little yard work for them. I sort of liked that better, because all that cash was mine. Do you have a problem with working?

Kevin: Not really, but I don't want to bus tables, wash dishes, or work in fast food places.

Uncle Joe: Well you have just eliminated a large portion of your work possibilities. What skills do you have?

Kevin: Skills? What do you mean by skills?

Uncle Joe: What abilities do you possess that someone would pay you for? For example, I'm planning on getting an electric car. Can you install the electrical outlet in my garage, that I'll need to charge my car?

Kevin: No.

Uncle Joe: Are you a wiz in mathematics or chemistry where you can tutor your cousin Frank?

Kevin: No. Are you trying to make a point?

Uncle Joe: Your asking that question tells me you get the point. The bible says, if you don't work you don't eat. I believe that especially applies to men. You might call me old school, but if old school information or instruction is correct, then it's correct. Knowing your parents as well as I do, they understand that a young man has to work. At some point you will determine what that work will be, but right now you need to get a job to learn things that only working or a job can teach you. I told you the story about FICA. If I really didn't want to have taxes taken out of my check, I could have my own business.

Kevin: You don't have to pay taxes if you own your own business?

Uncle Joe: You still have to pay taxes, but you literally pay them after you deduct the expenses for running your business. For example, let's say I have a lawn care business. I have a lawn mower, yard tools, gas, maintenance expenses, etc. I can deduct most, if not all the expenses needed in running my business. Let's say I made $2000 last week and I had the following expenses ($150/gas, $200/new weed eater, $100/lawn mower maintenance, and $20/business cards). That's $470 I would deduct from the $2000, leaving me with $1530. I would have to pay taxes on the $1530 and not the $2000. You actually can deduct a lot more than I gave in this example: Things that you would spend money on even if you didn't have a business. That's where you really see the benefit of having your own business.

Kevin: Oh, I see.

Uncle Joe: Your parents may be saying get a job, but what they really mean is do some work for pay. What you do is up to you, as long as it is legal, ethical, and moral.

Kevin: Yeah, because I know some guys who deal in pharmaceuticals who make some serious cash.

Uncle Joe: I know, that's why I said what I said the way I said it. I wasn't born yesterday.

Kevin: I wouldn't sell drugs anyway. I'm not trying to get hemmed up.

Uncle Joe: I never liked asking your grandparents for money. Once I started making my own money I experienced another level of freedom. When I wanted something, I went and bought it. If I didn't have enough money for the item I wanted I saved until I could afford it. I have always enjoyed my independence and working gave me a taste of it. That's another reason why I joined the military shortly after I graduated high school. I wanted to be independent of your grandparents.

Kevin: I don't know about joining the military, but it would be nice to have money of my own. The allowance I get doesn't go as far as it used to.

Uncle Joe: Allowance, what's that? You are a blessed young man. My parents didn't give us an allowance, nor did your Aunt Ann and I give Nicole and Dias one either. You are already getting free room and board.

Kevin: Man, I guess I am blessed.

Uncle Joe: It wasn't as bad for your cousins as I may have made it sound. Your cousins got just about everything they asked for and more. They just had to ask. When you get to your age, especially in the southern part of the country you are trying to get your driver's license. We provided them with a vehicle they could drive, but they needed money for gas, so they had to have their own money.

Kevin: I got my driving permit last week.

Uncle Joe: Once you get your license, next year you are going to want to go to your school's sporting event, things that you are involved in at school, dances, and all of that so it will be good to have money of your own.

Kevin: I wasn't thinking that far ahead. There are some things I wanted to do and haven't been able to because either I didn't have enough money or neither mom or dad could take me. Next year would you put in a good word for me so mom and dad will get me a car?

Uncle Joe: Sure, as long as you are working. You said something that is important for you to start doing.

Kevin: What's that?

Uncle Joe: "I wasn't thinking that far ahead." You have about three years left in high school, if you don't graduate early. You need to be thinking about life after graduation: What you want to do. Where you want to attend school. The type of schooling; be it trade school or college. This work thing is much more than you suppose. It is one of the first rungs on the ladder to manhood.

Kevin: Is it really that serious?

Uncle Joe: It may depend on the individual. The year and a half I worked at the restaurant taught me that I'll never work at a restaurant again. While I was working there they hired a guy as a dishwasher who looked like he was at least 40 years old. I thought to myself, once I leave this job I'm never going to do this again. There's nothing wrong with washing dishes, but I couldn't see myself having to do it more than twenty years down the road. I made a vow to myself, that whatever I had to do I wasn't going to be in this same position at this guy's age. I learned several other things as well, about myself and working for others: All of which has helped me become a more knowledgeable person.

Kevin: I'll go ahead and start looking.

Uncle Joe: You know that cookie place I like?

Kevin: Are you talking about that cookie store over where you used to live near the University?

Uncle Joe: Yeah. I think they are hiring. If they are, do you want me to get an application for you?

Kevin: Sure.

Uncle Joe: They know me and your aunt pretty well since we get cookies almost every weekend. I can put in a good word for you as well.

Kevin: That sounds good Uncle Joe, thanks.

Uncle Joe: This job thing might work out for you and me.

Kevin: How's that?

Uncle Joe: Their employees get discounts on their purchases. I'm sure you'll hook your good ole Uncle Joe up.

Kevin: We'll see...

SCHOOL

Uncle Joe: Hey Billy, your mom told me you got some Z's on your report card.

Nephew (Billy): You can't get Z's.

Uncle Joe: They may as well be Z's. You get the same amount of credit for it as you do for F's.

Billy: Ha-ha, that's not funny.

Uncle Joe: But no one's laughing. It's not funny. I was a student, a teacher, an administrator, a counselor, and I'm a parent, so no it's not funny at all. I know how intelligent you are. I've known you all 12 years of your life. I know you are brilliant when it comes to doing the things you enjoy, like sports, chess, board and video games, but when it comes to school work you do the minimum. I know your parents aren't pleased.

Billy: I only got one F and that's because that teacher doesn't like me.

Uncle Joe: I've probably heard that a thousand times. Why do you think this teacher doesn't like you?

Billy: She's always calling me out for stuff that other kids are doing too.

Uncle Joe: Like what?

Billy: Like if kids are talking, she's going to call my name.

Uncle Joe: When kids are talking are there ever kids who aren't talking?

Billy: Yeah.

Uncle Joe: Why don't you try being one of those kids for a change and see if she calls your name. If you believe someone doesn't like you, the best revenge is your success. So, if this teacher doesn't like you, make her give you an A. If she doesn't like you, you're giving her exactly what she wants, your failure. If you believe what you said your strategy is counterproductive.

Billy: But you don't understand.

Uncle Joe: What is it that I don't understand? Please explain it to me.

Billy: No matter what I do, she'll fail me anyway.

Uncle Joe: Have you tried my strategy before?

Billy: No, because I know it won't work.

Uncle Joe: Maybe I was wrong.

Billy: Wrong about what?

Uncle Joe: Your intelligence. If you believe what you just said. Teachers don't have time to hold personal vendettas.

Billy: What's a vendetta?

Uncle Joe: It's when someone holds something against a person and tries to make their life miserable because of what they said or did.

Billy: Yeah, she has a vendetta against me.

Uncle Joe: Boy I'm about to stop talking to you. So, what you are saying is because you believe this teacher doesn't like you, you're going to give her what she wants. You aren't even going to fight. So, you are okay with the grade you got?

Billy: No.

Uncle Joe: Then what are you going to do about it?

Billy: I'm going to get her fired.

Uncle Joe: How do you intend on accomplishing that? What evidence do you have?

Billy: Evidence?

Uncle Joe: Yes, evidence. I'm sure you have tests and papers that she graded where you turned in exceptional work, but she gave you whatever grade she wanted to. No doubt, you've aced tests, but she chose to count several of your correct answers wrong. I know your mom and dad are very involved in your schooling and communicate with your teachers regularly, so you may as well stop trying to convince me of this foolishness. By the way I know Mrs. Green. I worked with her several years ago and she is still the same sweetheart of a lady I knew her to be back then. So, this fairytale you've made up needs to stop, because you are only hurting yourself. Your parents and teachers don't work as hard as they do for students to fail. As a matter of fact, it's been my experience that all you have to do is go to school regularly, make a sincere effort to do all that your teachers ask of you and they won't let you fail. When I was teaching that was my philosophy. Some students, unlike you, have legitimate learning disabilities, but they gave their all. That kind of student would never fail my class. I would work with them. The only students who failed my class were those who decided they weren't going to do the work, study for tests, or just not come to school regularly. And then you know what happens?

Billy: They fail your class?

Uncle Joe: Yes, but that's not the saddest part of it.

Billy: Well you can fail so many classes and still go to the next grade.

Uncle Joe: Yes, that's true, but we are creatures of habit. When we make the decision that being mediocre and failing is okay, too many students carry that mentality into adulthood and wonder why they don't have the option of college, starting their own business, or even being able to go into the military, because they can't pass the military (ASVAB) test. I know what I'm talking about because I was a recruiter when I was in the military. A lot of young people couldn't pass the test to go into the military, because they didn't bother to learn much of anything while they had the opportunity.

Billy: Just because you tested a bunch of dumb people doesn't mean I'm dumb.

Uncle Joe: I guess that's my point. How do you know how smart you are if you just give up and stop learning because you say somebody, my teacher, doesn't like me? That doesn't make sense to me. You and a lot of other kids need to stop taking this free education for granted. We are so spoiled in this country. School is free, for the most part. We provide free bus transportation that comes in your neighborhoods every school day. Your education isn't limited to what the teacher is teaching. You can take college courses for free when you get to high school. You can take advanced classes in areas that you may be interested in. You can choose from a variety of electives: Learn how to sing, act, play an instrument, learn a trade like carpentry, masonry, electronics and more. I have had the privilege of visiting other countries where the only kids that go to school are those whose parents can afford it. Those kids are the ones who get the best jobs, go to college, and run the country. Those who are uneducated stay at the lower echelon of the socioeconomic level. They stay poor. You may say what's that got to do with me? I'm glad you asked. Both your parents are educated and do well financially. That's how you're able to live in this nice home. Food is always in the fridge and pantry, and you have a decent wardrobe. One day it's going to be your responsibility to provide for yourself and very possibly your family. What are you going to tell your wife and kids? Well family, if Mrs. Green had liked me when I was in the seventh grade, I would have made something of myself. I would have made better grades and become someone great, but Mrs. Green stopped me.

Billy: Nah, it wouldn't be like that.

Uncle Joe: I hope not. You need to stop looking at school and even life from an immature child's point of view, because before you know it you're going to be a young man and you'll need to know as much as you can. What kind of man do you want to be? A smart or intelligent man? A dumb or ignorant man? You hold the keys to your future. You can be whatever you want to be. You, unlike too many kids your age, have two educated parents who will help and guide you so you can get in and go to college, if that's what you choose to do. You have relatives who have had life experiences who don't mind sharing them with you.

Billy: Like you.

Uncle Joe: Exactly, see you are smart. Don't fall into this foolishness where you don't understand the importance of obtaining knowledge. The bible says, people who lack knowledge perish or are destroyed. I see it every day. Now that doesn't necessarily mean you have to have a formal education beyond high school, but you have to understand you need knowledge to be successful in life and it starts in school.

Billy: As soon as I graduate from high school I'm leaving this small town.

Uncle Joe: Why's that?

Billy: Because everybody knows everybody.

Uncle Joe: Okay, we'll let that be your motivation. Make sure you have every option available to you, like college, academic scholarships, military, maybe even start your own video creation business. The sky can be the limit if you use the brain God gave you and the resources you're blessed enough to have available to you.

Billy: Yeah, I'd probably be great at developing video games. I'm pretty good at playing most of them.

Uncle Joe: Let's go play. If I even come close to beating you, you'll need to reconsider your career plans.

EARLY CAREER PLANNING

Billy: That was a great game! LeBron must have scored fifty points.

Billy's Dad (Brother): I think he did.

Uncle Joe: Is this the first time you've seen him play, in person?

Billy: Yeah. Hopefully I'll get to see him play again before he retires.

Billy's Dad: We should be able to do that. You guys ready for this ride back to the house?

Uncle Joe: Sure, I'm just going to be sitting here.

Billy's Dad: Joe, your nephew and I have been talking about his plans after he graduates high school.

Uncle Joe: That's good. You're a freshman, right?

Billy: Yes, Sir.

Uncle Joe: So, what are you planning on pursuing?

Billy: I'm not sure yet. My high school puts emphasis on three tracks and we are to choose the one that fits us.

Uncle Joe: What are the tracks?

Billy: College, entering the workforce, and military service. We not only have to choose one of these tracks, but make a five and ten-year plan after graduation.

Uncle Joe: That's good. It makes you guys have to think about your future career options and what you'll need to do to prepare to take advantage of them.

Billy's Dad: Of course, I've shared my experience and I think it would be helpful for you to share yours as well Joe.

Uncle Joe: Sure...When I was your age, about 14, I planned on going to college. I thought I'd major in mathematics, engineering or something that was math related, because that had always been my strongest subject in school.

Billy: Did you consider a vocational track, like carpentry?

Uncle Joe: No. I took one electronics class, but that was as far as that went. I hadn't been exposed to any vocations really so I was ignorant as to what they were all about. I didn't learn how to work with tools and on varied equipment until I was in the Air Force. Like I was saying, I had planned to go to college and enter the Air Force through the ROTC program. Your grandfather thought it best that I attend the college closest to the house so I could stay at home and save money. That made a lot of sense, since it was his money and the university had AFROTC. I really didn't want to continue living at home so I enlisted in the Air Force instead.

Billy: But I thought you wanted to go to college.

Uncle Joe: And I did, while I was in the military. The thing about making plans is that they can change. As you talk to different people, discover other possible options, and are introduced to opportunities your plans can flex. Sometimes you have to make turns as life's roads demand. You'll see this happening all through my story. So, I joined the Air Force. It took me several years to complete my baccalaureate degree, primarily because I didn't know what I wanted to do. My first job in the Air Force was working on aircraft armament systems and their support equipment.

Billy: You probably did well in that, the way you can work on cars and stuff.

Uncle Joe: No, that's how I learned how to fix mechanical equipment. When I first started I didn't even know the names of some of the most basic tools. The military provides its airmen and troops with excellent training. So, I was taking classes and I thought I'd become an accountant, until I took my first accounting class. I thought it would just be numbers and doing a variety of calculations, but I found out I had to learn a different language, which I wasn't interested in doing.

Billy: What do you mean a different language?

Uncle Joe: I learned, as you will, that every job and career uses words that pertain to that job or career and in order to communicate effectively, you have to learn the language. Even at your school algebra, biology, and English use words that are specific to the subject.

Billy: Okay, I see what you mean. You have to learn the words that they use to communicate. That's been one of my struggles in algebra, but I'm getting used to the words the teacher is using, so it's becoming easier for me to understand what she's expecting from me. That's the first time I've ever heard it put that way.

Uncle Joe: So, accounting was out. A few years earlier I had re-trained and become a recruiter. This was one of those turns in the road. Well actually it was more of an intersection where I could choose which way I wanted to go. I chose recruiting. Recruiting is associated with Human Resources, so I changed my major to HR, which was another turn in the road.

Billy: So, you knew you would make the military a career?

Uncle Joe: No, I came very close to getting out, right before I made rank, because it was taking me so long to get my next stripe. Fortunately, as my paperwork for discharge was being processed I got my fifth stripe. It would have been a big mistake, if I had gotten out. I didn't have a degree, nor did I have a concrete plan as to what I was going to do. Thank God things happened the way they did.

Billy: I thought you liked being in the military.

Uncle Joe: I did. Like most people, at some time or another, your Uncle Joe was trippin. I had had a situation that caused me to get into my emotions and not think rationally.

Billy: Sort of like when I wasn't doing well in Mrs. Green's class a couple of years ago?

Uncle Joe: Yes. It's just a human condition where our response to other's actions, especially those who are in authority over us, hurt our feelings or treat us unfairly, and we make decisions that affect us in a negative way. It happens all the time. We have to think beyond our hurt, emotions, pride, and even anger and do what's truly best for self. If you don't remember anything else said in this conversation, remember to never make decisions based on your emotions. It will rarely, if ever, work out for your good.

Billy: Yeah, you were right about Mrs. Green. I was trippin.

Uncle Joe: That's how it is sometimes. We need to be honest with self, swallow our pride and keep moving forward. Now on rare occasions there are some teachers whose maturity level doesn't rise much above that of the students they teach, which is terribly unfortunate. I may not have made that admission in that conversation, but yeah Mrs. Green is "good people." Alright, so, where was I?

Billy: You didn't get out of the military, did you?

Uncle Joe: No, I stayed in, completed my degree and retired. I thought I'd become a pharmaceutical rep and sell drugs legally for a few years, but that didn't work out, so I went to plan B, which was teaching AFJROTC in high school. This was another turn in the road. I had spent some time in JROTC classrooms while I was a recruiter, so I was somewhat familiar with what they did. It was a good transition into education. I did that for five years, in two different locations. Your Aunt Ann and my first AFJROTC instructor colleague encouraged me to apply for a principal fellowship and to my surprise I got it. This was a no brainer. It was a door to becoming an administrator where the state paid me to complete a master degree in school administration in two years. I couldn't turn that down. I was an assistant principal for eight years and did a couple of other jobs in education before deciding to retire early.

Billy: You got tired of the crazy kids?

Uncle Joe: The kids or students were the easy part. The more challenging issues were with the adults: teachers, staff, and parents.

Billy: I might consider teaching. I think I'd make a great PE teacher and coach.

Uncle Joe: Yeah, I know you love sports, but do you love people?

Billy: I love some people.

Uncle Joe: The reason I asked that question is because the best educators (teachers and coaches) love not only what they do, but the people they have the pleasure to interact with on a daily basis. Education is a people business and there are too many people doing it who don't even like kids. At least that's the way it appears, outside looking in.

Billy: Yeah, there are some teachers who you know don't care about you.

Billy's Dad: I had a couple of them when I was in school. If I had listened to them I wouldn't have gone to college, because they talked like it wasn't for me. Luckily, I was around other people who believed in and encouraged me.

Uncle Joe: So that has been my career so far, but I'm not dead yet. I have plans to do a variety of things between now and the end of my life. There is still much to learn, places to visit, and lives to touch. I have only just begun. So, has this conversation helped you at all.

Billy: Yeah, I think so. It's helpful to know I don't have to know everything now. Whatever I decide to do may not be a life sentence. I may be able to do a lot of different things, like you did.

Uncle Joe: Brother, what did you learn?

Billy's Dad: I learned a new way to get to the house. During all this talking I missed a turn and had to take a different route.

Uncle Joe: Well you know I have to get my beauty rest. It's hard to maintain all of this manly handsomeness without proper sleep and relaxation.

Billy's Dad: Fortunately for you we're only a few minutes away, cause judging by the way you're looking you've been missing a lot of sleep lately.

Billy: Dang dad, that's cold.

Uncle Joe: That's how your dad is, but as his older brother I forgive him.

Billy's Dad: The truth is what makes us free, my brother.

Uncle Joe: Now he's trying to use scripture. Forgive him Lord for he knows not what he saith.

Billy: Amen.

TODAY'S ISSUES

Niece (Connie): Thanks for taking the time to talk to me today Uncle Joe.

Uncle Joe: No problem. Anything to help. So, what's going on.

Connie: I'm writing this paper for my civics class. I'm combining empirical research with surveys from a few people and I thought of you.

Uncle Joe: Okay, sounds good. I'm ready when you are.

Connie: Great. I have a few topics that I'd like to get your opinion on. We'll start with "Black Lives Matter."

BLACK LIVES MATTER

Uncle Joe: Black lives matter, that's true. Asian lives matter. White lives matter. Hispanic lives matter. Native American lives matter. Mexican lives matter. All lives matter. I really am ashamed as to how people in power have responded to the Black Lives Matter movement. It's obvious to me that what folks are saying is Black lives matter too. They aren't saying that their lives matter more than any other life, of any other race of people. They are saying that we matter too and want to be treated with the same dignity and respect as White people. During the recent protests throughout the country and even around the world, I was happy to see a collection of all races of people represented in this movement, especially so many young people. We, as a nation, have an opportunity to make reforms in our judicial system, to really employ justice for all. The question is, what will we do with this opportunity?

Connie: Why do you think there is so much opposition to the Black Lives Matter movement from the top of our nations' government?

Uncle Joe: I think those who are in power fear losing their power. They see this movement and the changes in our nation's population as a threat to their power. I think it unfortunate, but it reveals this idea of superiority and an unwillingness to share power. The problem with this type of thinking is today it's race that is the thing that separates us, tomorrow it can be hair color, eye color, religious affiliation, political party, personal beliefs, differences of opinion. No one is safe. It is just a matter of time before you become the target, no matter how safe you think you are.

Connie: Okay, the next subject is racism.

RACISM

Uncle Joe: Racism is one of the most irrational ills in our society. It's crazy to think of myself greater or better than anyone else. None of us had a choice in who we are as far as race and ethnicity. I didn't determine my race. I didn't choose my American parents. I didn't choose the time-frame I would be born. None of that was my decision, yet I think myself better than someone else? How crazy is that? In my estimation, racism shouldn't exist, especially in America, at least not like it does. The only people who might have an understandable right to have issues with race in America are Native and African Americans. Native American's land was taken from them and their culture all but destroyed. African Americans were taken from their home land and brought across a vast ocean, in unthinkable conditions and enslaved for hundreds of years and still suffer injustices daily. We should be in a much better place regarding race in this country, but it won't happen as long as people think they don't have a dog in the fight. Just like I mentioned regarding the Black Lives Matter movement, today it might be Mexicans, tomorrow it could very well be you.

Connie: Okay, what's your take on civil rights past and present?

CIVIL RIGHTS

Uncle Joe: Civil Rights...It is a sad state of affairs that we have yet to settle this really simple problem in America. I remember as a small child in the 60's seeing people who looked like me and you being beaten by police, doused with water from powerful fire hoses, and bitten by police dogs on the evening news. These things weren't happening to them because they were being violent, but because they were protesting the inequalities of the time. I also remember liking a little light skinned girl in my neighborhood. We were the same age and couldn't have been any older than 5 years old, because we hadn't started school yet. We were swinging in one of those basket-like swings, facing each other and I asked her if she was White. Her answer to that question, be it yes or no, would not have changed the way I felt about her, but I understood, in my young innocent mind, that if she said she was White the possibility of us having any type of relationship beyond distant friends was most likely. She said, with a snaggle tooth smile, "no, I'm not White." I felt a sense of relief at her answer, knowing that society would not object to our being together. There will always be those who object to you, whoever "you" are (Black, female, poor, etc.) as being equal to an imaginary standard or expectation, but our laws must never condone this mentality. When laws are in place to keep a segment of our population in "their place" we have infringed on their civil rights. I guess the question is, is that who we as a nation choose to be? The answer to the question of civil rights is very simple. Do unto others as you would have them do unto you. I think this biblical principle is the antidote for every topic you've asked about thus far. We just need to have the will to do and enforce laws equitably.

Connie: Now, what do you think about defunding the police?

DEFUNDING THE POLICE

Uncle Joe: Defunding the police is not the answer. We need the police. All of us need to be able to call on a police force of good, honorable men and women for our protection. The issue is getting rid of the rogue cops. It's really that simple. One of the major problems is the lack of courageous leadership to make the necessary changes. When I started my military career, I worked around nuclear weapon systems. We were told that if we were transporting a nuclear weapon and were overtaken by enemy forces, foreign or domestic, our lives would be in jeopardy.

Connie: What do you mean?

Uncle Joe: One nuclear weapon can kill hundreds of thousands, even millions of people, depending on the density of the population in the area. We knew that if we lost control of a nuclear package we were as good as dead, because it's better to lose a few military members than hundreds of thousands or millions of people. The bottom line is they, our own comrades, would take us out with the perpetrators. What that meant is my life and the lives of those in charge of protecting this nuclear weapon, depended on our ability and will to use deadly force to protect it. If someone had tried to get control of the weapon, they would have been blown away. We understood the reality that our lives were on the line and we'd use deadly force to stay alive. The culture of our police forces needs to be such that they know, should they commit a crime, they too will suffer the consequence for their action(s). Misconduct will not be tolerated.

Connie: Are you saying they should be killed?

Uncle Joe: No, no. I'm saying that there should be no question in their mind that their actions will have specific consequences, based on the law, that they have sworn to uphold. If they commit a crime like shooting an unarmed person, disregarding a person's civil rights, making up bogus charges, any crime, they are subject to the laws of the land just like any other citizen. They are subject to losing their job if they are deemed to be unfit even if they haven't committed what one might consider a crime, but if they are abusing the powers and authority that policing requires. There also needs to be additional training in how to deal with a variety of situations. You don't shoot first and ask questions later. You don't make assumptions that just because a person looks a certain way that they are a criminal. There needs to be a shift in their mindset. For example, when I was an assistant principal, I dealt primarily with students who had behavioral issues. After a period of time, if I hadn't stepped back in personal reflection, I could have begun to believe that most of the students were "bad kids," when in reality the vast majority of students are good kids. Even the kids with issues weren't bad, but had circumstances that they needed assistance in overcoming. So again, the police don't need to be defunded. They need to get rid of the "bad apples," revamp the training, and change the culture to truly protect and serve all communities equally.

Connie: We're almost finished.

Uncle Joe: I'm retired. I can always do tomorrow what I have planned for today.

Connie: Our next topic is Colin Kaepernick.

COLIN KAEPERNICK

Uncle Joe: I actually admire him. I think he was simply protesting the problem of police brutality and the injustices he believes exist in his community of black and brown people. Why didn't we listen to him? Why did we bring military service members into the mix of the conversation? Why did leaders in our nation's highest offices decide to make comments about, what one could consider, a trivial action? I know why he knelt or took a knee during the national anthem, because I listened to his explanation. As a retired military member and an American, who was born and raised in this country, I wasn't offended. I understand that he was using his platform to draw attention to these injustices. I see it as his right as an American citizen. He didn't make any obscene gestures or make any noises that interrupted the playing of the national anthem. Why was this blown out of proportion? I think it's because there are some people who really either don't know what democracy is or looks like or don't care to know. They want to define it for us. We are supposed to have freedom of speech, but there are those who want to minimize the voices of some people whose "speech" doesn't align with theirs. Is that democracy? They want you to comply with their worldviews, their likes, their dislikes and as long as you do, they'll tolerate you. But don't have an original thought. Don't speak or act before you ask for their permission or they'll have a problem with you and get others on their side to silence you, if they can. Our entire conversation today has been about this faulty mindset, that if you don't look a certain way or act a certain way you are wrong and we won't tolerate it or you. You will be subject to our way or else and the else could very well mean death, literally. That doesn't sound or look like democracy to me.

Connie: Okay, Uncle Joe our last topic is COVID 19.

COVID 19

Uncle Joe: COVID 19 is a horrible virus that has caused millions of people their lives around the world. It is unfortunate that we, as a nation, haven't collectively taken it seriously. If we had I believe we would be on the other side of it. What this virus has done is revealed the hearts of many people, especially those who are in leadership. Many leaders haven't taken it seriously, putting the almighty dollar above people's lives. Then you have people who are so concerned with their individual freedoms that they could care less about the health and well-being of anyone else. Some religious leaders have shown their hand, in that they don't have a problem putting their congregation's health in jeopardy and the government can't tell them what to do and not assemble. This virus will probably be history in the next several months, but from what I have seen what we should have learned from it will be lost to far too many people. This was an opportunity for Americans to come together as one, regardless of religion, race, political view, gender, and fight an enemy that doesn't discriminate, but we failed. Instead, COVID 19 has revealed how sick our nation really is spiritually, emotionally, morally, and ethically. In order for us to recover, we must first acknowledge our sickness and seek the proper antidote. I am hopeful that this virus will meet its fate in the next several months. My real concern is for the transformation of the hearts of mankind. That is what will make the long-term difference.

ACKNOWLEDGEMENTS

This book, nor anything else can be accomplished without God, my Heavenly Father, The Great I Am, the God of Abraham, Isaac, and Jacob. I don't want there to be any confusion about the God I am referring to. God has been so faithful throughout my life. He continues to lead and guide me to new heights and accomplishments. He's made my life a true adventure. I look forward to the next expedition. Thank you, Lord.

To my deceased parents, John Wesley and Ida Mae Peek, for doing all they knew to do to raise their children to be productive citizens. My admiration for them grows stronger daily as I reflect on all they provided for us, in modeling good character and godliness.

My wife, Toni, whose love, support, and encouragement gives me the courage to embark on the next assignment God has for us. You are truly my better half.

Lastly, to my adult children (Christian and Jonathan) who are living their independent lives in a way that inspires me. There is nothing you can do to make me stop loving you.